POST-
MAN

POST-MAN

essays on being a neuro-divergent non-binary person

ALEX MANLEY

ARSENAL PULP PRESS
VANCOUVER

ARSENAL PULP PRESS
Suite 202 – 211 East Georgia St.
Vancouver, BC V6A 1Z6
Canada
arsenalpulp.com

The publisher gratefully acknowledges the support of the Canada Council for the Arts and the British Columbia Arts Council for its publishing program and the Government of Canada and the Government of British Columbia (through the Book Publishing Tax Credit Program) for its publishing activities.

Arsenal Pulp Press acknowledges the xʷməθkʷəy̓əm (Musqueam), Sḵwx̱wú7mesh (Squamish), and səlilwətaɬ (Tsleil-Waututh) Nations, custodians of the traditional, ancestral, and unceded territories where our office is located. We pay respect to their histories, traditions, and continuous living cultures and commit to accountability, respectful relations, and friendship.

Arsenal Pulp Press is committed to reducing the consumption of non-renewable resources in the making of our books wherever possible. We make every effort to use materials that support a sustainable future. This book is printed on paper made with 100 percent sustainable recycled fibre content.

No AI was used in the making of this text.

The following essays were previously published in different form:
- "The Lead Essay" (as "Get the Lead Out") in *Hazlitt*, October 29, 2020
- "Have a Good One" (as "Will That Be All?") in *Maisonneuve* 53 (Winter 2015)
- "Behind the Masc" (as "Will There Ever Be an Openly Queer NHL Player?") in *The Walrus*, January 12, 2021
- "The Rat's Tale" (as "Business in the Front, Rebellion in the Back") in *Catapult*, June 15, 2021
- "I Grow Old, I Grow Old" (as "Facing Bald") in *This Magazine*, July–August 2022

Every reasonable effort has been made to contact copyright holders of material reproduced in this book. We would be pleased to rectify any omissions in subsequent editions should they be drawn to our attention.

Lyrics from "Refusing to Be a Man (Different Studio Version)" are reprinted with permission of Propagandhi.

An excerpt from "The Moment I Saw a Pelican Devour" from *Space Struck* (2019) by Paige Lewis is reprinted with permission from Sarabande Books.

Lyrics from "King Park" are reprinted with permission of La Dispute.

Cover design by Jazmin Welch
Text design by Riley Simmons
Typesetting by Jazmin Welch
Edited by Catharine Chen
Proofread by Alison Strobel

Printed and bound in Canada

Library and Archives Canada Cataloguing in Publication:
Title: Post-man : essays on being a neurodivergent non-binary person / Alex Manley.
Names: Manley, Alex (Poet), author
Identifiers: Canadiana (print) 20250144913 | Canadiana (ebook) 20250147483 |
ISBN 9781834050126 (softcover) | ISBN 9781834050133 (EPUB)
Subjects: LCSH: Manley, Alex (Poet) | LCSH: Neurodivergent people. |
LCSH: Gender-nonconforming people. | LCSH: Neurodiversity—Social aspects. |
LCSH: Gender nonconformity—Social aspects. | LCGFT: Essays.
Classification: LCC PS8626.A5568 Z46 2025 | DDC C814/.6—dc23

Some people know who and what they are fairly early on.
This book is for the rest of us.

A battle hymn to celebrate
the fact that we don't have to become
or remain what we've come to hate.
—Propagandhi, "Refusing to Be a Man (Different Studio Version)"

There is no guarantee that everyone will see you clearly. Who carries the mirror? Who is your true witness? You, beloved, must see yourself. They may cast you as anything. That does not make you that thing. Have you met yourself? Do you know who you are?
—Aleah Black, @gendersauce, Instagram

Contents

The Lead Essay

FOR ME, THIS STORY STARTS IN THE FALL OF 2020, with a loose collection of tweets.

Even into the third decade of the twenty-first century, Twitter was still seen as being the future of news by many, but one thing I'd discovered by then was its paradoxical tendency to communicate users' often oblique reactions to breaking news before the news itself, leaving you to patch together the details like a digital detective.

Did two people tweet contextless YouTube links to songs by the same legendary musician within five minutes of each other by pure coincidence? Was it their birthday? Or was I going to find a link to a hastily typed obituary a few tweets down, a TMZ headline, a slew of crying emojis and hearts?

In this case, the first tweets I see are straight news sent out by a handful of journalists I follow, people who worked at the student newspaper I cut my teeth on in college. It's late November right now. No one seems to be tweeting reactions just yet, but maybe that's because it's a news story that sort of defies the easy reactions Twitter is so good at channelling.

Montreal has a lead pipe problem.

Not like Mr. Boddy in a game of Clue (I accuse Shoddy Plumber, in the Sewer, with the Lead Pipe) but like municipal inspectors screwing with the lead-testing numbers, steadily jimmying the figures downward, like a tenant struggling with a leaky faucet. Drip. Drip. Drip. Recorded parts-per-billion numbers have been significantly off. In reality, they're likely way above legal limits. Buildings all over the city are affected—houses, schools, restaurants. We are drinking tainted water. Have been for some time now.

So used to turning the tap and watching the water come out, like magic. But as with any sleight of hand, it's what you don't see that you should be thinking about.

It's hard to know how to respond to the news. Friends of mine resort to a kind of watery gallows humour. I send an email to the people I'm hosting for my poetry workshop: I have various beers, white wine, Canada Dry, almost every kind of hard liquor, and good ol' Montreal-brand Tap Water™. Ha. Ha.

Not long after, Twitter user @tomzwar does get off a reaction tweet of note, going micro-viral with this joke, mistaking, as many North Americans do, the parodic tone of a generic, bumbling twentieth-century Frenchman for something more universal in Francophonie:

> Montréal people be like: Sacré bleu! Ze pipes at ma polyamoureuse partnér's apartment are poizoned with lead[1]

No one in Montreal sounds like this, but the third accent aigu, the *z* in *poizoned* and the *-euse* ending grafted onto *polyamorous* are just aurally specific enough to make it a minor hit both within and without the island, garnering many hundreds of likes.

Not long afterward, my partner, who's just moved to Montreal from Toronto, sends me a picture of an empty shelf in the downtown Canadian Tire. Brita water filters that filter out lead are sold out.

/

With Montreal's lead pipe problem on my mind, I start to find references to industrial poisoning everywhere, a toxic Baader–Meinhof phenomenon.

In a 2011 essay in *The Nation* entitled "Why I Call Myself a Socialist" by the actor Wallace Shawn, retweeted onto my feed by an American Bernie supporter:

1 esprit de toad (@djtoadfish), "Montréal people be like," Twitter, November 10, 2019, https://twitter.com/tomzwar/status/1193412226989744128.

"Around 400,000 babies are born on earth each day. Some are born irreparably damaged, casualties of the conditions in which their mothers lived—malnutrition, polluted water, mysterious chemicals that sneak into the body and warp the genes."[2]

In a book I'm reading, Anne Boyer's *The Undying,* the author's daughter saying, in response to news that her mother's cancer is not genetic: "You forget that I still have the curse of living in the world that made you sick."[3]

A few pages earlier in the same book, in a poem by Diane di Prima: "1. kill head of Dow Chemical / 2. destroy plant / 3. MAKE IT UNPROFITABLE FOR THEM to build again."[4]

A writer I follow on Instagram posts a story of a Wikipedia page on long-term nuclear waste warning messages. Ideas on how to protect future humans from our radioactive waste after we're gone. Suggestions include hostile architecture, a sort of maze designed to spit you out in one place rather than another. And a text to ward off future wanderers, translated into "every UN written language." It, too, is a type of poem.

> This place is a message ... and part of a system of messages ... pay attention to it!
>
> Sending this message was important to us. We considered ourselves to be a powerful culture.
>
> This place is not a place of honor ... no highly esteemed deed is commemorated here ... nothing valued is here.
>
> What is here was dangerous and repulsive to us. This message is a warning about danger.
>
> The danger is in a particular location ... it increases towards a center ... the center of danger is here ... of a particular size and shape, and below us.

2 Wallace Shawn, "Why I Call Myself a Socialist," *The Nation*, February 3, 2011, https://www.thenation.com/article/culture/why-i-call-myself-socialist/.

3 Anne Boyer, *The Undying: Vulnerability, Mortality, Medicine, Art, Time, Dreams, Data, Exhaustion, Cancer, and Care* (Farrar, Straus & Giroux, 2019).

4 Boyer, *The Undying*.

> The danger is still present, in your time, as it was in ours.
>
> The danger is to the body, and it can kill.
>
> The form of the danger is an emanation of energy.
>
> The danger is unleashed only if you substantially disturb this place physically. This place is best shunned and left uninhabited.[5]

On YouTube, the algorithm recommends a trailer for a movie called *Dark Waters* about DuPont poisoning a small town. A *New York Magazine Intelligencer* article by Max Read about the seemingly inevitable creep of facial-recognition technology circles back around to lead:

> There's no corresponding fatalism around regulating (or prohibiting) technologies that aren't computer networks. Most states and cities maintain bans on particular kinds of dangerous weapons, for example. Or take a deadly substance like lead, which used to be discussed in not-unfamiliar terms of indispensability and inevitability: "Useful, if not absolutely necessary, to modern civilization," the Baltimore Afro-American wrote in 1906, years after it was first clear that lead was fatally toxic. Even decades later, lead was still touted as an inevitable constituent of the future: "One of the classic quotes from a doctor in the 1920s is that children will grow up in a world of lead," historian Leif Fredrickson told CityLab recently. Not unsurprisingly, it took the U.S. decades longer than the rest of the world to eliminate the use of lead paint indoors. But still, we banned it.[6]

Canada banned lead paint in 1960, beating the US by nearly twenty years. But a latticework of lead pipes still connects the city's municipal drinking water sources to houses all over Montreal.

Properly executed tests show numbers of up to 15 parts per billion, three times the federal legal limit. Because I live in a building built before 1970, it

5 Kathleen M. Trauth, Stephen C. Hora, and Robert V. Guzowski, *Expert Judgment on Markers to Deter Inadvertent Human Intrusion into the Waste Isolation Pilot Plant* (Sandia National Laboratories, 1993), https://digital.library.unt.edu/ark:/67531/metadc1279277/.

6 Max Read, "Why We Should Ban Facial Recognition Technology," *Intelligencer*, January 30, 2020, https://nymag.com/intelligencer/2020/01/why-we-should-ban-facial-recognition-technology.html.

might be in my pipes, and in the pipes of my downstairs neighbours. I think of the young family with the baby who moved out from under me last summer. I watched her change into a toddler while she smiled up at me from the backyard garden below my balcony. How many glasses of water did she drink? Did her mother pour for her, or for herself? Can lead poisoning be passed on through breast milk? I wonder.

If something is banned but doesn't go away, what does it become?

/

One of the things that lead exposure can do to people is impact their ability to focus.

In the summer of 2019 or 2020, after a conversation with a friend, I began to suspect that I had undiagnosed attention-deficit issues. Doing some research into the subject, I discovered many new things about ADHD, tics and quirks and accretions of habits and feelings that fly under the radar. Over time, I learned about things like rejection sensitivity dysphoria. Frequently needing to wash one's hands while cooking. Spilling small amounts of water when drinking. Most importantly, I learned that ADHD is not, as it is often framed, a complete inability to focus; rather, it's a struggle to focus in specific instances. That is, those with ADHD can focus on things that interest them without much—if any—difficulty; it's work and matters of study and conversations they find boring that lead to the stereotypical mind-wandering. I think back to all the years I spent at university, trying and failing to marshal my mind through the tasks in front of me. How many essays I started after midnight, the day they were due.

Now, I find that there's something almost anti-capitalist about ADHD. You can't focus on anything but the things you find naturally engaging; your mind can't easily be yoked into service for drudgework at school or in the workplace. You're a sort of wild horse: just as fit as the tame ones for running at great speeds, but of no use to farmers, plowmen, carriage drivers, or knights errant. In short, a horse as it was meant to be, not a horse as we have come to imagine them.

That's not to say that people with ADHD are perfect, untainted by the ills of capitalist progress, but to a certain degree, any form of neurodivergence is cultural in nature—it's an attempt to frame why someone does not meet our expectations of how a person should be.

But that is not a fixed concept, and as such, neither is mental illness. So what, exactly, are we medicating?

In the spring of 2018 I began taking anti-anxiety medication for the first time. A few months later I upped my daily dose from 20 mg to 30 mg a day. Around that time, I ended a nearly four-year relationship and began a whirlwind summer of flirting, dating, sexting, and hookups.

By September, three different people had told me they no longer felt comfortable being my friend due to things they'd seen or heard about me doing that summer. I reduced my dose of fluoxetine from 30 mg a day to 20 mg a day, and started seeing a therapist.

I say this because, even before the lead, I'd spent the last year and a half thinking regularly and at length about the relationship between the self and the substance, the impact that certain chemicals have on our brains, the impact that these substance-altered brains have on our actions.

If we are what we do, what we do is informed by the chemical makeup of our brains, and the chemical makeup of our brains is impacted by the things we eat, drink, breathe, apply to our skin, and live on, under, inside of, or around, then what is the self?

As Terese Marie Mailhot says in her memoir *Heart Berries* of her struggles with depression, "I couldn't distinguish the symptoms from my heart."[7]

The things I did, the people I hurt, the friends I alienated, how much of that was 10 extra mg per day of liquid fluoxetine? How much was three and a half years of sexually frustrated monogamy preceding that summer? How much was growing up in a city with doctored lead-water numbers? How much was being socialized as a straight white male? How much of it should I own, how much should I eat?

/

Before this year, I was most familiar with cognitive decline from stray fragments of culture—*Benjamin Button*, "Flowers for Algernon"—and from my own persistent anxieties, which would swell up and die down periodically, that I myself was experiencing it.

These worries were not typically tied to anything in particular, did not engender any behavioural changes on my part to prevent my own worsening, but they cropped up over and over. I became adept at hunting down signs I could use as proof to bulwark against the nagging in my head that said,

7 Terese Marie Mailhot, *Heart Berries* (Counterpoint, 2018).

You're not as sharp as you used to be. You're not as smart as you should have become by now.

Over the winter I played Scrabble against my paternal grandmother—a game and a half—and demolished her in what used to be a somewhat competitive rivalry. In the lengthy pauses between my own quick turns, I had time to wonder, *What will it feel like when I, too, begin slipping away?*

A sort of sluggishness. A glazing over of the eyes, watching an inevitability take shape.

/

It's a Friday in November and I'm staying at my partner's place all day to accept delivery of a furniture order from Structube—a grey Nora ("reconstituted wood veneer 4-drawer chest," $249), and a black Trevor ("set of 3 aluminum and iron nesting tables," $149).

As I do about once a day during this period, I come across yet another tweet about lead. Not about Flint, Michigan, whose water has been unsafe for drinking due to elevated lead levels since 2015, but this time about the lead in another American city: Baltimore, a nine-hour drive south of Montreal.

> Baltimore has reached the 300 homicide mark, but again, you won't find the mainstream media actually examining root causes. Like the fact that toxic lead exposure is an ongoing crisis in the city and should be declared a state of emergency.
> It's like science doesn't matter.[8]

One of the replies to the tweet says, "So it's because of lead that baltimore has the 20th highest murder rate in the world? Not buying that one …"[9]

I wonder if Baltimore is different from New York or Washington or Philadelphia, and if so, how. I come across a map of the city showing where the lead remains and where it isn't. A shape cut into the map that doesn't touch the poor parts of Baltimore. They call it the "White L" and the "Black Butterfly." Steps in a dance. I think about Freddie Gray in the back of the van.

8 @BmoreDoc, "Baltimore has reached the," Twitter, archived November 15, 2019, at https://web.archive.org/web/20191115113741/https://twitter.com/BmoreDoc/status/1195302245224583168.

9 Mateo (@mvpielli), "So it's because of lead," Twitter, March 7, 2019, https://twitter.com/mvpielli/status/1103716555148255232.

The original tweet, by user @BmoreDoc, is quote-tweeting another tweet. I click through and read the original tweet he's responding to, from user @BmoreLEADfree.

There's a link to an article on Medium entitled "Baltimore's Ongoing Lead Poisoning Crisis & the Link to Violent Crime." I click through and begin to read the article. "It's impossible to talk about crime and violence in Baltimore without talking about the thousands of youth that have been hurt by the neurotoxin of lead. Further, nearly all victims had no access to medical, behavioral, or nutritional therapies."[10]

Next, I read the Wikipedia page on the "lead–crime hypothesis" and a doctoral thesis by Jessica Wolpaw Reyes entitled "Environmental Policy as Social Policy? The Impact of Childhood Lead Exposure on Crime."

It argues convincingly that the Environmental Protection Agency's move to reduce the levels of lead in gasoline starting in 1973 is in large part responsible for the significant drop in violent crime across the United States over the past half century or so. That lead poisoning is known to cause impulsive behaviour, to lead to aggressiveness, to impair cognitive functioning.

It argues that the visible fall of blood lead levels in America happened in concert with the fall of violent crime. It argues that the problem is more pronounced in big cities. That the impact is significantly more severe on poor communities where people live densely and closer to the street. The source of car exhaust.

I think about who is poor in America. What they look like and where they live. I think about *Escape from New York*. I think about *RoboCop*. I think about George H.W. Bush's attack ad against Willie Horton. *We considered ourselves to be a powerful culture.*

I keep reading. I learn about the CDC's slow but steady jimmying downward of what a healthy amount of blood lead is. I am becoming familiar with the phrases *micrograms per decilitre* and *blood-brain barrier*. I think about the dose of dextroamphetamine I took in the morning, which is making me more focused.

After reading up on ADHD for a bit, I was able to convince first myself and then my doctor that I probably do have it. I've been taking one or two pills on days when I need to focus on work stuff. Sometimes it helps. Sometimes I spend several hours focusing on unrelated matters. On Wikipedia I come across information about the history of lead. I keep reading.

10 Lawrence Brown, "Baltimore's Ongoing Lead Poisoning Crisis & the Link to Violent Crime," Medium, September 10, 2018, https://bmoredoc.medium.com/baltimores-ongoing-lead-poisoning-crisis-b53870c4a142.

/

In the lead-up to the 2019 federal election, the leader of Canada's New Democratic Party, Jagmeet Singh, is asked whether he is offering a "blank cheque" to First Nations communities with regards to fixing their drinking water, something incumbent Liberal Prime Minister Justin Trudeau has made little progress with in office. Boil-water advisories are still in effect in dozens of towns and reserves across the country, and Singh has promised to address the issue if he becomes PM.

"Are you just writing a blank cheque for all problems across all Indigenous communities across the country once you get into office?"

"So, if Toronto had a drinking water problem, if Montreal had a drinking water problem, would you be asking the same question?"

"It's a lot of money, is what I'm saying. And people will look at it and go, 'How much money are we going to spend on all this? How are you going to find that money?'"

"That's a genuine question. Would you be asking this question if Vancouver did not have clean drinking water? Would you be asking this question if Edmonton did not have clean drinking water? No, you wouldn't. That's what I'm saying. Why is it that we ask the question about whether or not Indigenous people should have clean drinking water? We've got to take a minute and think, *Why is that even a question?* Yes, they deserve clean drinking water! Yes, we can make it happen! It's a matter of priority, and I'm going to do it."[11]

I vote for the NDP candidate in my local riding. She loses to the Liberal candidate; after two terms in orange, the riding is now red.

Later, when the news breaks about our water, I wonder if Montreal is different from Edmonton or Toronto or Vancouver, and if so, how.

/

The way we move around online is a fascinating thing. The internet is a series of tubes, a system of pipes, a means of delivering things. But it can also feel like a maze designed to spit you out in one place rather than another.

Some websites let you read about a man named Thomas Midgley Jr., who, in the employ of General Motors in 1921, discovered that adding tetraethyl

11 "'Why Is That Even a Question?' Singh Vows to End Boil Water Advisories in Indigenous Communities," Global News, October 5, 2019, https://globalnews.ca/video/5995008/why-is-that-even-a-question-singh-vows-to-end-boil-water-advisories-in-indigenous-communities/.

lead to gasoline could fix an automotive problem specific to GM cars called "engine knocking." Another lets you read about a Russian boy who claims he was born on Mars talking about the Sphinx. One of the medical websites I'm on keeps showing me clickbaity links to it.

After a few hours, my curiosity gets the best of me. I google some of the terms involved. The claim is that there's something behind the Sphinx's ear. I end up on a Reddit thread, then on an article from the Smithsonian Museum's magazine that talks about an American man's hunt for the secrets of the Sphinx.

The article talks about the wear and tear the Sphinx has been subjected to over the years. Someone hypothesizes that ancient Egypt was once much more temperate and humid than it is now, how over centuries the forests gave way to sand. I envision the Sahara ambling back through the jungle, a prowling figure in the night. What that must have been like to see.

The article also talks about the building of the Sphinx and the pyramids. It says according to archaeological evidence, it's likely the workers were eating prime beef—the bones of young bulls were found in their dwellings—so they probably weren't slaves.

I wonder what's more likely, that the middle class was casually rotating in and out of doing back-breaking labour in gigantic architectural vanity projects, as the article suggests, or that the god-king thought steak-fed slaves would produce better results? I accuse Mandatory Overwork, in the Desert, with the Whips.

Anyway, I think, it's a moot point. If you're spending your time doing unpaid labour building the sphinx, it doesn't matter what social class you come from or what you eat. It's just an expansion of what the term *slave* can be used to describe. *We considered ourselves to be a powerful culture.*

I think about what my friends and I eat. And how many of them have money—savings accounts, retirement funds. Whether anything any of us builds will last as long as the plastic containers we throw out after a meal. I get back to the lead.

/

The Wikipedia entry on the lead–crime hypothesis is darkly fascinating, but one quote in particular calls out to me from the Background section: "Dioscorides would later report that 'the mind gives way' in individuals exposed to lead."[12]

12 "Lead–Crime Hypothesis," Wikipedia, archived June 30, 2021, at https://web.archive.org/web/20210630071436/https://en.wikipedia.org/wiki/Lead%E2%80%93crime_hypothesis.

Something about the specific tenor of the phrase resonates in me. The idea of the mind, like the ground beneath us, giving way—an earthquake, a landslide, a collapse. To give way is both a passive action and a violent one. It, too, is a type of poem.

I start to google, looking for more context around the quote.

I come across a story of a little boy in St. Louis. It takes me the better part of fifteen minutes to track it down—the Google hit I click on doesn't lead me to the quoted passage and, ultimately, I have to find a cached version on the Internet Archive—but in 2014, a St. Louis–based medical journal published a Patient of the Week story about a seven-year-old boy involving lead. Phrases jump out at me.

He had two episodes of emesis the night prior and five on the morning of
Two were streaked with small amounts of blood.
+fatigued lately, but dressed
himself that morning, Mom
worried mostly about the blood in his
vomit.
Asthma, ADHD, Anemia, diagnosed 3 weeks ago
He was difficult to arouse.
Abdomen was soft.

complicated by acute blood
loss (recall the hematemesis).

Waxing and waning mental status in ED continued.
Respiratory distress, then respiratory failure developed.
intubated pulmonary edema.

declining mental status.

A flat plate of the abdomen is shown below:
The radiopaque material in the GI tract (paint
chips) suggested lead poisoning, and the
diagnostic test was sent.

Blood level 104 mcg/dL (normal is zero)[13]

13 Line breaks/erasures my own. "Case Study: Not Just Vomiting," Children's Hospital St. Louis, archived May 15, 2015, at https://web.archive.org/web/20150514055242/www.stlouischildrens.org/health-care-professionals/publications/doctors-digest/june-2014/case-study-not-just-vomiting.

I scroll down a bit further, and there's a short essay on lead by a doctor named Ashish Doshi. It begins, "Lead is among the first metals to be mined and used by humans, owing to its low melting point, malleability and corrosion resistance."

Doshi's essay quickly sketches the route that lead takes from mines to the mouths of babes.

Greek physician Nikander discovered   toxic effects of lead   2nd
century BC   he observed colic   paralysis   century later
Greek physician Dioscorides wrote   "The mind gives way."

the introduction of lead-based residential paint   19th
century brought lead within reach of children. The addition of tetraethyl lead to gasoline
1920s to   1980s   contributed to lead
exposure   contamination of air, dust and soil.   physicians made
connection between lead-based paint   toxicity in children   early
1900s.

Lead-based paint   banned   most of the developed world   mid-1930s,
aggressive lobbying   U.S. Lead Industries Association prevented   U.S. ban
late 1970s.   lead industry   campaign   discredit the studies   began
featuring children   in their advertising.
In   St. Louis, 90 percent of housing
built before lead paint was banned.

Later:

There is no known safe level of lead and no apparent threshold for physiologic effects.[14]

/

14 Line breaks/erasures my own. "Case Study: Not Just Vomiting."

I think about something else I read about St. Louis, in Patricia Lockwood's memoir, *Priestdaddy*. She writes of the children she grew up with. I scan the passage. Here, too, phrases jump out:

> why were so many of us limping, feeble, milk-white, ill? There
> were kids
> stunted by rheumatoid arthritis, who had fragile walks
> pink pinpoints on their knees and knuckles
> One boy's eyes so clouded he was
> nearly blind: Asthma
> infertility rare cancer clusters, girls with cysts all
> over their ovaries. A preponderance of twins, one sickly
> one well. Rashes of stillbirths
>
> Babies born missing eyes, missing ears, conjoined. No one
> knew why.[15]

Eventually, she discovers that the local landfill contained nearly nine thousand tons of radioactive waste from the Manhattan Project. What kind of evil is it to see destruction and do nothing? Who is worth protecting, if not children? *The danger is still present, in your time, as it was in ours.*

/

When I was a child, I used to hold my breath around cars.

My parents must have told me that car exhaust was bad—we didn't own one at the time and never would; to this day neither myself nor either of my parents nor my younger sister has ever owned a car as long as I've been alive.

I remember once coming across a car with two separate tailpipes, one on each side of the rear bumper, and feeling a deep spring of hatred well up inside me. What monster would want to emit twice as much poison?

I still hold my breath when cycling through a visible cloud of exhaust. I don't how much good a few seconds of not inhaling one particular patch of smoke does me when stacked up against living in a major city's downtown area for three

15 Line breaks/erasures my own. Patricia Lockwood, *Priestdaddy: A Memoir* (Riverhead Books, 2017).

decades. And I worry that the sharp inhale I take upon exiting the visible exhaust cloud might draw in more toxins than simply breathing normally would have. But there's no one, really, to tell you what the right approach is.

That's the way it is with a lot of things that are bad for you, I feel. There's not a specific line where it's too much—we just kind of accept that it's bad and we shouldn't. And we go on with our lives, pushing the bad thoughts down.

Me, I avoid certain things: smoking cigarettes, vaping, antiperspirants. I've heard that too much processed meat could give you cancer, and holding in your bowel movements could increase your chances of colorectal cancer, the bacteria leaching into your skin.

I used to worry about microwaves, what they were doing to my food. For years after I got comfortable using them I still thought it wasn't safe to microwave margarine. But googling it a few years ago turned up nothing. How many things am I uselessly afraid of?

Scrolling through end-of-decade best-of lists, I re-encountered the trailer for the 2011 Terrence Malick movie *The Tree of Life*. There's a scene in it that perfectly captures this horror: a troop of laughing children running and dancing through the fog of pesticides being sprayed on their parents' idyllic 1950s lawns, suburban mid-century Americana distilled to its purest essence. Technological progress, the removal of the unsightly other from the picture, the slow, steady poisoning of innocence. Those children, just like St. Louis boy, living their lives in a capitalist hellscape, their brains and bodies slowly betraying the presence of evil, the proverbial snake in the green grass of the backyard garden. I wonder if any of them held their breath.

/

Of course, natural things try to kill us. Lead is just a piece of the Earth that we started pulling up out of it. If we're honest with ourselves, the planet is hostile. For a certain strain of person, it's tempting to chalk toxicity up to human machination and to plunk healthful living down in the realm of the natural.

But for every human-engineered exhaust pipe and PVC toy, there are poison dart frogs and tsetse flies, water-borne parasites and radium. Would all these people trying to eat paleo trade places with their forebears to escape the chemical haze we live in?

I think often, like Max Read, about banning certain forms of technological progress. What do we really need that we don't already have? Would we not benefit from grinding the gears to a halt, returning to the Earth?

My partner and her friends have been joking about starting a cult lately, buying some land out in the middle of nowhere, and I get it.

/

One of the songs I most associate with a certain strain of early 2000s culture—a song I never had on a CD or in an iPod or computer but which I fell under the spell of each time I heard it played—was the Deftones track "Change (In the House of Flies)." It's haunting and beautiful, intimate and cruel, feminine energy in a masculine package, the type of song you might hear between tracks by Linkin Park and Static-X and the Alien Ant Farm Michael Jackson cover on a certain strain of radio station or Spotify playlist that seems nevertheless to far outstrip the artistry of its peers' creations.

It's of this song I think, of course, when I first read about the House of Butterflies.

The phrase crops up in an article I'm reading about leaded gasoline, a fuzzy scan, a black-and-white Xerox of a text from the mid-twentieth century, and like "the mind gives way," it, too, is a type of poem.

I google the phrase *house of butterflies* and find an article by Rebecca Skloot called "Houses of Butterflies," published in the University of Pittsburgh's alumni magazine, about a scientist named Herb Needleman.

Needleman talks of his experiences as a young man working alongside men who'd been employed at the DuPont Deepwater Works in New Jersey, where tetraethyl lead was mixed with gasoline:

They called it the "House of Butterflies" because the workers began to hallucinate. They could see flashes of living colour in the air where there weren't any, an insectarium of the mind. Snatching at nothing.

The things the human mind does with incomplete or corrupted data are fascinating. Does the sound of a needle skipping on a warped record count as music? A leadened brain conjuring flapping wings not once, not twice, but over and over and over, in five men, ten men, twenty. Men who are in the process of dying. Some of whom will be in straitjackets soon.

I think of the 1997 animated movie *Anastasia*, where the title character chases brightly coloured butterflies in a dreamy haze, unaware that she's on a ship, wandering perilously close to the edge, sleepwalking up to the mouth of death, the yawning sea.

Needleman's experiences with the workers from the House of Butterflies were instrumental in his railing against the lead industry later in life. His scientific work then instrumental in getting lead banned. "Lead does so many things to human biology, we don't even know which ones are most important," he says in the alumni magazine interview. It affects neurotransmitters responsible for nerve conduction, causes leaky capillaries, kills brain cells, affects RNA transferase and transcription of the genome, and that's just an abbreviated list. "There are thousands of articles out there," he says, "and so many effects that could be critical, we don't really know what's what," and then he pauses. "We just know that the more you look for brain effects, the more you find them, even at very low doses."[16]

I check the date on the UPitt article. It was published in 2001. I check the date of St. Louis boy's Patient of the Week story. It is from 2014. St. Louis is a nine-hour drive west of Pittsburgh.

I wonder if any copies of that issue of the UPitt alumni magazine ever made it to St. Louis over the course of those thirteen years. Mailed to former graduates who'd returned home. Stuffed in a milk crate with old copies of *The New Yorker* and *Harper's* by someone who got a job there. Left under a seat on an intercity bus.

I wonder what year that leaden paint was applied in St. Louis and by whom, who chose it in the hardware store, whether any of the paint in that store on that day was lead-free. The processes by which things are invented, designed, created, built, packaged, shipped, stocked, advertised, sold. Capitalism is a system of pipes, a means of delivering things.

Every few months, it seems, a retweet about the water in Flint arrives on my digital doorstep. It's been five hundred days since Flint had clean drinking water. It's been a thousand days. It's been 1,500 days. Tweets note how little of various billionaires' absurd hoards it would take to rectify the issue. I read articles. I watch videos. The same nothing continues to happen.

Recently I came across a *Mother Jones* article in which a writer argues vehemently that there's no proof that drastically declining reading comprehension levels in Flint's students has anything to do with the city's leaden water. The security blanket of plausible deniability.

Before COVID-19 enveloped America like wildfire licking at the country's lungs, exploiting loopholes in the country's backward and broken health care system like a hacker making quick work of a shoddily constructed website's lax security, it was already a dangerous place to be powerless, a place governed by a sort of nationwide bystander effect. All the people with power in society waiting for someone else to do the heavy lifting, to pick up the phone and call for help.

16 Rebecca Skloot, "Houses of Butterflies," *PittMed* 3, no. 1 (January 2001), https://www.pittmed.health.pitt.edu/story/houses-butterflies.

I remember, in early 2017, reading in the *Atlantic* that experts predicted a pandemic emergency could do unprecedented damage to the world because Trump's administration would be particularly ill suited to responding to one.

I remember, as a teenager, reading in *The Atlantic* that experts predicted a powerful hurricane could do unprecedented damage to New Orleans. I think now of the way these tragedies unfold in slow motion, until suddenly they're full-grown.

Is there anyone less powerful than the children of the poor, the Black and brown? What kind of evil is it to see destruction, and do nothing? Even when the destruction is slow, and quiet, and hidden away. What is it like to watch your children change, touched by that heavy substance lurking in the pipes, coming out as water, coming out as exhaust? Who is worth protecting, if not children?

/

In 2007, under the auspices of my first-ever writing workshop at Concordia University in their now-infamous creative writing program, I submitted a poem for critique entitled "The HMS *Terror*." The second half of it read,

> {i suppose it's fitting that
> lead poisoning was also known
> in times past as saturnism
> because (not because of the rings, no)
> of all the adjectives
> and there are many
> that describe depression
> arguably the most well-suited to the case
> is saturnine}

Like many poems written by nineteen-year-olds, it's really about being sad after a breakup, but I filtered the sadness through the fact that I'd been on Wikipedia reading about Franklin's attempt to discover the Northwest Passage, a voyage derailed in part due to the fact that the sailors' food rations were stored in lead tins.

Now, I think about the men going crazy in the frozen north. I wonder if any of them saw butterflies.

/

My maternal grandmother died in 2012. I accuse Cigarette Smoke, in the Throat, with the Carcinogens.

We never really got close until after the diagnosis, when I was in my early twenties. The sense that she was poisoning herself was intractable from my first interactions with her. The smell, the way it tinged things with an unhealthy yellow. The way she was always slipping away for a smoke break.

They first discovered that cigarettes were dangerous in the 1960s. According to the CDC, tobacco use causes over seven million deaths a year worldwide; each day, they say, three hundred people not yet old enough to legally purchase cigarettes become daily users.

Who is worth protecting, if not children? It's a sort of sluggishness.

/

I think about people stumbling upon six hundred tombs in Egypt for the workers tasked with building the Sphinx. I think about the twelve dead men in tetraethyl labs in New Jersey. I think about one near-dead child in St. Louis, a mass of lead collected in his guts. *This place is not a place of honor.*

To have a body, to be alive, is to be subject to capitalism. It touches us before we even come out, a probing finger, a bias that shapes an argument, a framework that demarcates what is and isn't possible. Casualties of the conditions in which their mothers lived.

/

In the Trump era, one of my favourite pieces of internet culture is "Mister Gotcha," a webcomic strip by Matt Bors featuring a run-of-the-mill white Twitter guy popping up throughout history to critique those agitating for change. The comic reaches its apex—and punchline—with the orange-T-shirt-clad jerk popping out of a well to respond to an emaciated medieval serf's complaint that "We should improve society somewhat." On cue, the smirking reply comes: "And yet you participate in society. Curious! I am very intelligent."[17]

The underlying logic perfectly captures the trap of existence: We are all—St. Louis boy, pregnant mothers, GM workers, all of us—born into a cage, a series of dangers laid out to ensnare us by forces beyond our awareness, understanding, or control. Pregnant British women taking their prescribed

17 Matt Bors, "Mister Gotcha," The Nib, September 13, 2016, https://thenib.com/mister-gotcha/.

thalidomide, American children bringing handguns to school, state-of-the-art airplanes going down in Ethiopia.

Our ancestors were born to die by predators. We are born to die by products.

/

One of the links on the Wikipedia page for Thomas Midgley Jr., the inventor of both tetraethyl lead and chlorofluorocarbons, is to a *Time* magazine feature from 2010: "The 50 Worst Inventions." I glance down. The next invention on the list is the "vibrating ab belt."

I try to imagine the kind of mind—or, considering this is a magazine, collection of minds—that could conceive of a list where the failures of leaded gasoline and the vibrating ab belt could possibly sit next to each other. What would an America poisoned and ruined by vibrating ab belt use look like? *What is here was dangerous and repulsive to us.*

A note near the end of the entry says that Midgley Jr. died from strangulation after getting trapped in a contraption he'd built. There is a saying about living by the sword, I think.

/

I remember a comparison I read once, that Americans are confused by the fact that Beijing has such a pronounced smog problem they somehow haven't been able to solve, but Chinese people are confused by the fact that America has such a pronounced gun problem they haven't been able to solve.

I think about how easy it was for General Motors to solve the problem of engine knocking, by comparison. I think about the fact that the problems that get solved are the ones that make someone somewhere rich, and the problems that don't get solved are the ones that keep someone somewhere rich.

I think about the phrase *If it ain't broke, don't fix it* and the two meanings of the word *broke.*

A population slowly losing its mind over the potential ills of vaccines—a medical technology with hundreds of years of positive results to its name—and yet silent about the enormous amount of lead that remains in American houses—a toxin with thousands of years of negative results to its name—has a clear set of priorities.

/

Eating non-food objects is known as pica. It remains a relatively poorly understood disorder, affecting primarily children and pregnant women, and is often associated with mineral deficiencies.

It's hard for me, reading up on pica, not to think about the relationship between the body and the brain more generally, the way specific needs get translated into desires. The foods, the drinks, the feelings we crave. How much of what we ingest is choice and how much of it is the brain reiterating the body's most pressing needs into the language of the grocery store, the fast food menu, the open fridge?

In the Patient of the Week article, it says St. Louis boy was anemic. How tasty chips of lead-based paint must look when you're seven and your body is missing vital stores of iron. A need you can't understand or voice pushing your hand toward the flaking spot on the wall. Peeling it off and wondering to yourself.

A medical info page tells me people with pica won't volunteer that they've been eating ice, dirt, rubber bands. They themselves don't understand what's happening—they're simply the middleman between brain and body.

/

How long does the bad thing stay? There's a Vox explainer video about the nuclear waste issue that I watched a few months before coming across the accidentally poetic text on Wikipedia that gets at this.

The idea that our forays into the powers of things that can kill simply by being near you is something we must reckon with, knowing they will outlive not just us, not just our descendants, but our culture entirely.

What would St. Louis boy's life have been like if we had the means to warn unwitting people about the presence of deadly toxins in their walls?

I'm joking, of course. The people who made the daisy chain of interlocking decisions that removed lead from the ground and spread it all over the walls of the house in St. Louis spoke and wrote the same language as the boy's parents.

Unlike future civilizations wandering, blissfully ignorant, into our long-forgotten yet still potent toxic waste, the barrier here is not one of language, nor of cultural understandings of danger.

Rather, it's a sort of sluggishness—having faith, perhaps, that something might be done, but neither the strength nor the inclination to set it in motion, like a dying person staring at a telephone a few feet away from them on the floor as the blood slowly drains from their arteries. A glazing over of the eyes, watching an inevitability take shape. *We considered ourselves to be a powerful culture.*

/

What do we worry will affect us?

At the end of a poem called "The Moment I Saw a Pelican Devour" by American writer Paige Lewis in their debut poetry collection, *Space Struck,* I find a discourse on the interplay between chemistry, sexism, class signifiers, and workers' rights:

> not even our mouths belong to us. Listen, in
> the early 1920s, women were paid to paint radium
> onto watch dials so that men wouldn't have to ask
>
> the time in dark alleys. They were told it was safe,
> told to lick their brushes into sharp points. These
> women painted their nails, their faces, and judged
>
> whose skin shone brightest. They coated their
> teeth so their boyfriends could see their bites
> with the lights turned down. The miracle here
>
> is not that these women swallowed light. It's that
> when their skin dissolved and their jaws fells off,
> the Radium Corporation claimed they all died
>
> from syphilis. It's that you're telling me about
> the dull slivers of dead saints, while these
> women are glowing beneath our feet.[18]

On Twitter I read that America has the rightmost major political party in the world. I wonder what the effect of several decades of tetraethyl lead inhalation on a country's collective consciousness might be like. How conservative and angry all the old people in North America seem to be. The phrases *OK boomer* and *brain worms* crawling all over social media.

I'm helping my partner paint her bathroom millennial pink, trying not to breathe in too much.

18 Paige Lewis, "The Moment I Saw a Pelican Devour," in *Space Struck* (Sarabande Books, 2019).

/

Scanning the City of Montreal's information page on the lead problem, I come across this paragraph: "*Si vous n'êtes pas en mesure d'effectuer cette vérification, communiquez avec votre propriétaire ou avec un plombier. Toutefois, même si votre entrée d'eau potable n'est pas en plomb dans votre domicile, il est possible qu'une portion souterraine le soit.*"[19]

My eyes notice something.

plombier

plomb

Plombier, plomb. Plumber, plumb. Leader, lead. It's hard to miss.

Later, when trying to re-find the quote to include it in this piece, I realize that plumbing itself is *plomberie*. They all come from the Latin term for lead, *plumbum*. In French, where the two words are closer, it's more obvious, but the very concept of plumbing is literally inexpressible, unthinkable, without lead.

And it is useful, after all. The work of the people protecting us from nuclear radiation also unthinkable without it. The chest apron for the dentist's X-ray. The lining of coffins at Chernobyl. Fight fire with fire. The enemy of my enemy is my friend. So malleable. Just like us.

/

When they are done bringing the Structube boxes into my partner's apartment, I offer the delivery men a glass of water. The shorter one is audibly out of breath, and accepts.

I go to the kitchen and turn on the tap. Like magic, the water begins to come out. *The danger is still present, in your time, as it was in ours.*

19 "Comment Reconnaître une Entrée d'Eau en Plomb," Montréal, June 14, 2023, https://montreal.ca/articles/comment-reconnaitre-une-entree-deau-en-plomb-19804.

It is being told by a woman "You're one of the good ones." A good man, a rare thing. But I'm not. I'm not one of the ones at all. How much I hated hearing it, how much I flinched. It is liking to wear flowers in my hair. It is gender as statement of allegiance. It is being part of the bridal party at a Sikh wedding in 2017 and getting permission to join in with the girls' tradition, getting hennaed. Little beautiful patterns on my skin, which lasted for weeks, made me feel pretty. It is battling with myself about whether coming out as non-binary is cowardice, whether I'm leaving behind narrow ideas of gender rather than burrowing into more expansive ones. Turning tail rather than standing and fighting. But I never was a fighter.

Have a Good One

THE CORNER STORE WAS IN SHAUGHNESSY VILLAGE, a little west of Montreal's downtown core. Though it's long gone today—replaced by a dumpling place that's since gone out of business too—it had been around for more than a decade when I was hired in May 2010. At night, there were bars on the windows and door, iron grates that each opening shift had to remove and each closing shift had to replace to keep the place safe when it was empty, exposed as it was on busy Rue Sainte-Catherine, with all its strange, enticing wares behind the glass.

Ostensibly, it was a magazine and newspaper shop; the racks featured a wide selection of titles from around the world and carried publications for every kind of taste—*Harper's* and *Harper's Bazaar,* the *National Enquirer* and *Lapham's Quarterly, Playboy* and *Farmer's Almanac, Der Spiegel* and *Paris Match, Runner's World* and *High Times, Artforum* and *Scientific American, The New York Times* and the *New York Post.* And if a customer couldn't find what they were looking for, the owners would order it.

But since magazines and newspapers have such small profit margins, the store also carried other items—some that you'd expect to find at a corner store, and others that you wouldn't. There was a helium tank for balloons, for instance, and a selection of dusty, aging greeting cards; an incense corner; a sad little basket of birthday and tea candles; and for a while, a selection of high-end pet food. We also had pipe tobacco, rolling tobacco, three humidors' worth of cigars, and a panoply of rolling papers. Meanwhile, the front window displayed pepper spray, knives, and even extendable steel batons, and behind the counter, there were cupboards filled with stacks of international calling cards that sat next to pouches of salvia. We had a dedicated stock of Ben & Jerry's; we had pipes and bongs. We sold lighters and gave away matchbooks for free; out front, a giant sign advertised that the store carried fireworks. One thing that wasn't advertised, however, was the fact that we sold crack pipes.

/

The store was co-owned by two brothers, and they seemed wrought from a particular strain of fiction—semi-literary, semi-pulp—about post-eighties North America. One was blond and one was dark haired, and the blond one was affable and good natured, and the dark-haired one was perpetually grumpy and cynical. The blond one had done martial arts for years and wore his long hair in a ponytail. The dark-haired one smoked weed and hit on every woman who came into the store. But then, his brother did too.

They were both married with kids, and the blond one owned a dog, a White Swiss Shepherd called Everest that he kept behind the cash on weekday mornings when he was there, half guard dog, half conversation piece. They would shoot the shit with all the regulars, and laugh at many of them once they'd left the store. They were street smart, not book smart; knew the crooks and the angles, could charm the cops when they stopped by, and had figured out how to bolster business by selling those glass pipes to the neighbourhood's endlessly renewable resource, the users.

I'm not sure when exactly the brothers decided to break into the crack pipe market, but it wasn't long before I could see why they'd decided to stick with it. As far as I could tell, neither of them was into drugs that much, but they were making an incredible markup on the paraphernalia. On a newspaper, it was a matter of pocket change, but they could net ten or fifteen dollars off the sale of a single weed pipe or bong. The crack stuff, though, was the most appealing from a business standpoint. The target market was large enough, the competition low enough, and the buyers motivated enough to ensure a constant, steady supply of customers.

A crack pipe cost five bucks. Those who bought them called them stems—though I also heard them called glass, tube, pipe, ungodly, and, not infrequently, "one of those" or "you know what I want." "Gimme a stem," one of them would say, and I'd reach into a cupboard under the counter, below the cash register, and close my hand around one.

There was something oddly perfect about them, those little glass tubes, maybe four inches long or so, how they looked when you piled a bunch of them on top of each other, what a full box of them looked like, an opaqueness of translucence. Like getting high, maybe—when you pile them all up on top of each other, it starts getting harder to see your way through to the other side.

"Five bucks," I would tell them. Usually they had the money ready. Sometimes they'd try to bargain. "I just have four." "Can you spot me two dollars, chief?" Or they'd fish for coins in the take-a-penny dish to hit their total. Before long, I started going through the dish, fishing out the glints of silver. Dropping those back in the register.

/

The stems weren't the only strange thing about the place. Working there was a learning process, one in which my initial perception of the store was slowly overwritten by a grimier, truer self, shift by shift. For every seemingly normal, law-abiding person who stepped through the store's front door unawares, there seemed to come a litany of stranger customers. Not a week would go by, it seemed, without an eye-opening experience. It started with my first shift and didn't let up from there.

That first day, I noticed a man trying to steal Red Bulls from the drinks fridge. I caught him at the door and stopped him in the front doorway, got four cans back from him without a struggle. I felt proud of having foiled the low-level theft, but the next day, after looking at the security tape, one boss said he thought the guy might have taken as many as six from the fridge.

In retrospect, the cans he took might have been stolen cans to begin with, boosted merch my bosses had bought dirt cheap and were reselling. But I wouldn't know about that aspect of the store for several months more.

Despite my failure to recover all six of the Red Bulls, they didn't fire me, not that shift or any of the next three, when I watched a bunch of teenagers run out the door with the two packs of cigarettes and some salvia I'd left on the counter while my back was turned, when some teenagers grabbed a handful of Roman candles from the box we kept them in and ran out into the night to celebrate a Habs playoff victory, or when a guy pretended a bottle of Orange Crush was too expensive and mimed putting it back in the fridge, only to walk by the window, drinking from it, a few seconds later.

Getting stolen from three shifts running hardly gave the impression that I was reliable, but I got the sense that they knew to expect a rash of thefts every time they hired a new employee. The sharks in the neighbourhood knew that was the best time to try shit. Like: A guy called Bruce[20] convincing me to take a dubious-looking American bill, telling me he was friends with the brothers. One boss, later that evening, counting the cash, asking me why I'd taken a fake bill, said: "Bruce is the biggest con artist I know."

Bruce's con artistry extended to showing up trying to sell us stolen goods, a practice that was not unique to him. During my tenure at the store, people tried to sell me video games; a crushed-up speed pill; an X-Acto knife; "fifty-dollar" shorts; "hundred-dollar" leather purses, in case I had a girlfriend; wine (white and red); AA batteries; an electric razor; "lotions"; cellphones; meat; seafood; perfume; jewellery; gum; chocolate; clothing; and Red Bulls. The first fifteen or twenty times, I said no. But they did keep coming back.

/

In addition to selling stems, we also sold two other crucial pieces of a crack smoker's kit: screens and pushes.

The screens (also called Brillos, or eggcorned as *brûlots* by francophone smokers) were the filter in the crack-pipe cigarette, located a half centimetre from the end to accommodate the crack rock put into the end and lit. To make a screen, I learned, you buy a few dollars' worth of steel wool at the Dollarama across the street, get a minimum-wage employee to cut it all into quarter-sized chunks, sell them at fifty cents apiece, and make back forty or fifty dollars, half a dollar at a time. (I later heard the Dollarama stopped carrying steel wool. Rumour was it kept disappearing off the shelves.)

We also made pushes according to similar principles. They were skinny lengths of wood the width of a charging cable and a little longer than the stems, used to properly tamp down the steel wool into the pipe, which meant a better smoke. To make a push, I learned, you buy a pack of fifty shish kebab sticks, remove the pointy ends, then cut them in half. Poof. A hundred pushes at fifty cents apiece is fifty dollars. You don't see that kind of markup every day.

20 Names of individuals in this piece (and throughout the book) have been changed to protect their anonymity.

Because of the diversity of what we carried, the store had a pretty wide customer base. Or, more accurately, it had several different customer bases who each came for different things. There were the regulars who lived in the neighbourhood, often alone, and treated the store as a daily stop on a to-do list—stopping in for smokes, newspapers, and lottery tickets, or just to shoot the breeze. There were students attending nearby Concordia University moving into the low-rent apartments that made up the Concordia ghetto who needed fresh-cut keys. There were the tourists who'd wander in off the street to ask for things—directions, advice on scoring weed, soft drinks from the fridge. There were also the crack users.

The store was a microcosm of its home borough; half of the locals earned under $20,000 a year, according to the 2011 census. And when a neighbourhood is poor and racked with drugs, I learned, that manifests in different ways. Sometimes dramatic, like witnessing a theft or back-alley sex work; other times mundane, like not being able to buy steel wool at the local dollar store.

/

My first week on the job, a kid named Tim, a skinny little redhead with a disarming, crooked smile, came in looking to buy a crack pipe. Trouble was, he didn't have any money. He wanted to know if he could put down his pair of rollerblades as collateral and he'd be back in a few hours with the cash. He kept hounding me 'til I said yes, and when he was gone, I didn't see him again for another week or two, the rollerblades languishing behind the cash, a symbol of my naïveté on wheels.

The next time Tim showed, he had the money for a stem, but not the money he owed me from the first time. I told him to get lost until he could pay me back, kept kicking him out of the store until he stopped coming entirely. Maybe he figured out my schedule or maybe he found some other place to buy pipes. I figured the brothers probably didn't run the only corner store in the city that was smart enough to profit off the crack market.

My father had once told me never to trust a drug addict, that they'd tell you anything to get their fix, and it had stuck, for some reason or other, the way phrases fathers tell their children manage to stick with them somehow. Tim's rollerblades were my first hands-on experience with the maxim that would come to define, in different ways, much of the two and a half years I spent behind the cash at that corner store. After Tim, it didn't take many more instances of being burned by wheedlers and guys with good stories for me to stop bothering to trust the users.

I realized after a few months that the tension that existed between me and the people buying crack pipes wasn't just their fault, though. Part of the trouble was that I was touchy, prickly, a bit of a jerk about it. I had my hard-and-fast rule, the one thing I could cling to in the haze of the store's moral vacuum. If someone buying a popsicle or a magazine was short fifteen or twenty cents, I would let it slide like we were old pals. "Don't worry about it," I'd say, waving them off as I collected their change. "Don't worry about it." But if anyone was ever short trying to buy a stem or a screen, my face would harden. "You know the price," I'd say. "Come back when you got the money." It was a tough-guy persona that was at odds with my real personality; I hate confrontation above all else, but at the store, I transformed into someone new. It wasn't about the money, of course; it was about the principle. As slimy as I felt selling these people the tools they were building their highs with, being charitable about it felt like a bridge too far.

I made nice with everyone else, though. As one of the brothers told me when I got hired, politeness was of supreme importance at this job. What he was getting at was that the store held a bit of a special place in the neighbourhood. Regardless of who was behind the counter, people came to talk, and I found myself not unlike a bartender—a fake friendliness, a propensity for listening, a little nod when I needed to move on to the next person. There were the old gay men who hit on me, called me beautiful, used innuendo, suggested we get a hotel room together somewhere. There were the gamblers, each with their favourite betting poisons. There were the drug users and the con artists, the old guys who bought the same porno mags every week. There were the guys who came just to talk and didn't buy, who told me about their lives for half an hour or an hour at a time while I took care of paperwork behind the counter. They were my neighbours, and for some reason, they seemed to trust me.

The only one I ever really trusted was Jimmy, though.

/

I met Jimmy during my first week on the job. I think he was in his early twenties, though his beard and worn-down clothes made him look older. The pleading look in his eyes, however, always reminded me of a child.

Everyone in the neighbourhood seemed to know Jimmy, one way or another. He would roam around our section of downtown Montreal, greeting strangers with a repeated chorus of "Ma'am, ma'am!" and "Bro, bro!," singular in his determination, unafraid to ask anyone for a bit of change. Over and over I watched kind souls try to help him. People bought him meals, or candy, or cans of Coke, which he seemed to prefer to solid food or even clothes. One time a man dropped off a pair of winter boots for him at the store, saying Jimmy had told him we'd keep them for him, and we did, though I couldn't help but wonder if he'd just wind up returning them for the cash.

Because, despite these acts of kindness, from my side of the counter, Jimmy's life appeared to have developed into one big funnel. Strangers gave him coins, which he traded to me for bills. He would then use the store's phone to call a dealer and arrange a meet. He then traded the bills for crack. Then he smoked the crack. Then he started over.

Given all the ways in which he was a poster child of what NIMBYS consider to be undesirable, I'm not exactly sure why the store was so friendly to him, why we let him use our phone, why we let him trade dirty change for clean bills, why we sometimes fronted him advances. But he did pay them back, did insist on it; he was the most trustworthy person I ever sold a crack pipe to, and he had a natural insistence and a natural innocence, a kind of Gollum quality that made him hard to say no to.

Over time, I guess, my bosses had given up trying to keep him away, whatever the impact of his frequent presence on the store's image, and that attitude slowly filtered through to each new hire. We just kind of lived with him. In some strange, tenuous sense, we were in community with each other. Though most of our interactions happened across the store's counter, because I lived only a block away, we ran into each other on the street fairly often. Whenever we did, he would stick his fist out to me, and I always fist-bumped it. Fifteen years before I'd hear the term, he was one of my unhoused neighbours.

/

They say you shouldn't take your work home with you. I can't say that I did, exactly, but the job changed me. Even part-time, some jobs just work their way into the fabric of you, like a strange new metal added to the melting pot. You come out not yourself but an alloy.

Though it's true that I was something like a bartender, over time, I watched myself change into something else, as well: a kind of cop. Maybe it was because so many of the store's customers were criminals, but I would find myself sorting out who to trust and who to scrutinize, developing a shorthand, profiling.

Slowly watching my even-handedness erode. There's something human about this; whatever your job is, over time, it's hard not to resent the people who cause you the most trouble. Before I knew it, a part of me started to venerate the people who made my job easy, almost pleasant, even, the people with whom I might accidentally fall into conversation with about an article in the latest *Atlantic Monthly* or laugh with about whatever the weather was doing now. Those people bought my good humour with their credit cards, their faith in the posted price of things, their reliability.

But there was also something sickening and racist about it. When the regulars—the white regulars—complained about the neighbourhood going downhill, homeless First Nations people loomed large in their minds. I would wince, listening to their casual bigotry. But I also knew the job had curdled some prejudice into my own thoughts. I didn't agree with them, but I never pushed back, either.

And if I was a cop, then I was a crooked one. I don't remember what it was that made me change my mind about stolen goods, but eventually I realized what my bosses had realized: That at some point it doesn't make sense to turn down something that's a tiny fraction of the price, right in front of your nose and still in the wrapping. I didn't buy much—a bottle of Absolut from the nearest SAQ, some Toblerone bars around Christmastime. As far as I could tell, the store was just a stop on the route these guys took once they'd boosted something—anything—that could be considered, by anyone, to be of value. I don't know what kind of person would buy Armani perfume from a street hustler, but if the thieves didn't think they could sell it to someone somewhere, they wouldn't steal it in the first place.

On my bosses' behalf, though, I was less choosy. For them, I bought steak, freshly taken from the supermarket a block over, and alcohol—rum, wine, Dom Pérignon, on New Year's Eve. Most of the buying was for the store itself, not the owners, though—Red Bull, gum, chocolate bars. Sometimes I engaged in bargaining. I'd call up the blond brother—he was the entrepreneurial one—and describe the goods being offered, and he'd make an offer or tell me to pass. Twenty cents per pack of gum. Ten bucks for a full box of chocolate bars. It was easy money for the thieves, and it tended to turn around nicely for the store, although some things I bought—like the box of Dollarama Mars bar knock-offs called Meteors—gathered dust.

Buying stolen goods was just one of the ways I found the job altering me for the worse. One of the guys who used to steal stuff to sell was a tall, good-looking, dark-haired Québécois type, fast talking, the kind of kid who could have been an entrepreneur or a lawyer or an actor if he'd come up in the right circumstances but who ended up being a desperate, angry, threatening junkie, who'd cajole and threaten when I didn't want to buy what he'd stolen, who'd beg and argue and wheedle. One time we got into a shouting match in front of a lineup of customers. Something about the job brought out my indignation and self-righteousness when people tried to pull a fast one on me or push my goodwill a little too far.

I got into probably half a dozen altercations like that over the two and a half years I worked there, sometimes over a quarter or less, each time leaving me sweating, my heart pounding, worrying about whether the guy would come back or, as one threatened, be waiting for me at the end of my shift. It was a job that I eventually realized would stay with me long after I no longer stood behind the counter, even after I stopped running into my old regulars, could no longer remember which smokes they took, even after I stopped having those work dreams, which I still have periodically to this day, still, at thirty-six.

/

Most of the people buying crack paraphernalia wanted to get in and out as fast as possible. They didn't want to be seen; they didn't want the other customers to know what they were there for. These buyers would hang back and wait until the store was empty, graciously letting a woman with a copy of *Chatelaine* go ahead of them in line so they wouldn't have to buy a pipe with a pair of eyes on their back.

They became easy to spot once I knew what to look for. It's true that some wore button-up shirts, pulled crisp bills out of wallets to pay for their pipes, and seemed untouched by the drug. Pre–Rob Ford, the idea of the suit-wearing crack smoker seemed absurd to me, but they did exist. The majority of the stem buyers looked more like what I'd expected, though. They wore saggy, dirty clothes. They were unkempt, with messy, unwashed hair, and often missing teeth. They were men and women, white and Black and Indigenous. Some were my age or younger. I sold stems to a few young men who could easily have been nineteen. Most were in their thirties and forties, though, and these ones usually looked the worst. If they'd been doing it for longer, maybe they hadn't experienced any semblance of a straight life for years and years. Once, I sold one to a woman who then asked, nonchalantly, which of the drinks in the fridge would be healthy for a pregnant woman. That was when

I noticed that the bulge under her shirt wasn't just a gut; that it was out of proportion with the size of her thighs.

Often I considered not selling crack pipes to them, telling them I wouldn't on principle or pretending we were sold out, but just like whenever a woman pushing a stroller came in and asked me for a twenty-pack of Peter Jacksons, I never ended up saying anything. It was their life, I would tell myself. *Let them sort it out. I'm not their parents. I'm just doing my job.* If it wasn't me, it would be someone else. And at ten dollars an hour, I sure wasn't being paid to care. Instead, I paid them the kindness of platitudes: I would try to tell them to have a good one the same way I said it to anyone else as they left, even though it made me feel empty. "Have a good one," I'd tell them. "Have a good one."

/

As I spent more shifts at the store, I got to know Jimmy a bit better.

He rarely bought pipes or pushes or screens; he mostly used the store for free matches, changing his coins out for bills, and calls to the dealers he hit up, the phone numbers always changing.

His relationship to the store itself was an interesting one. He would buy cans of Coke from the fridge, and stems periodically, but I wondered whether his frequent presence in the store might put off other customers. I told him repeatedly not to ask for change from people while inside the store, but his innate friendliness meant he often had trouble stopping himself from trying to strike up conversations with people. It wasn't begging per se, but it was hard to say where the line was drawn. I tended not to say anything. I never could stay seriously angry with him for long.

The stories I heard about Jimmy were that he had been a strong student in high school but had spiralled out of control a few years later and had been on the streets ever since. Someone said his older brother was a successful DJ somewhere, rich and famous, and Jimmy, the homeless crackhead brother, was a family embarrassment. Some claimed to have known him in his pre-crack days. One of my bosses worked out that, on a good day, Jimmy could pull in a hundred dollars or so, and all of it went to crack pipes, crack, and the occasional Coke can to keep him going. In fact, the last summer that I worked at the store, Jimmy showed me a hundred-dollar bill he'd been given, one of the new polymer ones, when they still felt new and high-tech. He'd crumpled it, like he crumpled all his bills. It was jarring to see something so nice and new treated no differently than the worn fives and tens he usually traded in.

Because of his shabby appearance, because he was a Black man in the streets, because he actively hunted down potential donors rather than sitting and waiting, some people told me that Jimmy scared them. But from the day I met him and asked him if he wanted an empty soda can I'd finished for the deposit, and he turned it down—it wasn't worth it to him to spend five minutes chasing five cents—I realized that unlike every other user I dealt with, he was honest and harmless to a fault, would pay me back if I advanced him a few dollars ("I always pay you back, man, I always pay you back, don't I?"), accepted it when I told him he wasn't getting the phone that day because I was in a bad mood. He always put his fist out, asking for props, when we ran into each other on the street, which we did often, during the day or at night, three or four in the morning, when he was still on his grind and I was making a late-night snack run to the twenty-four-hour depanneur, and as soon as he recognized me he stopped asking for money mid-sentence and just said, "Hey, Alex," and I'd say, "Hey, Jimmy," and he'd say he'd see me around, and that was that.

"I love you, bro," he told me on more than one occasion. "You know that, right? I love you." It broke my heart a little bit to hear it. I wondered briefly if he might have been gay; there was something sensitive about him that ran counter to traditional cishet masculinity. But it never sounded like the lust-driven advances I was sometimes the recipient of behind the counter. It just sounded like he didn't have anyone else, and the tiny bit of charity and frustration-diluted kindness I showed him was one of the nicer things in his life, in the shifting sea of faces not giving him the time of day. Or maybe he was just working me, trying to stay in my good graces so he could keep swapping change for bills, keep using our phone for free. I never could tell.

/

The store was never short on surprises, like the time I saw a man remove crack rocks wrapped in tinfoil from the holes in his gums where teeth used to be, or the time I discovered what I initially thought was a stash of cocaine, a dozen baggies that I estimated to be worth around $10,000, before a neighbourhood tough guy came in one day asking for a bag of the "fake coke" because he had tourists ready to buy. But perhaps the most surprising thing was how long I stayed. When every story I came home with sounded so seedy, my parents and friends didn't understand why I didn't quit. But there were upsides.

Outside of the crack stuff, and the fact that I was minimum wage or close to it the whole time, it was a great job. When my bosses left the premises early in my evening shifts, the place became my kingdom. It was a rare service job where I could spend my hours in the company of the written word, absorbing the best new writing on the continent for hours, shift in and shift out, flipping through the high-brow magazines, mainlining articles and essays and excerpts and fiction into my still-developing brain, the flow of beautiful and well-crafted sentences, punctuated by the little jingle of the bell that rang when the front door opened.

For a young person who always felt shy and not taken seriously, it was also nice to be in charge of something, even if that something was not exactly wholesome, even if everything in the store seemed to be tainted in some way or other. It felt good knowing things by heart—which brands of cigarettes the regulars smoked, how they liked to gamble. And when one of them would stay a while to chat, hearing their stories transmuted me from low-wage worker to confidant, an ersatz corner-store talk therapist.

Of course, the unofficial perk of snacking on chocolate bars each shift didn't hurt either. And the crack stuff wasn't so bad, really, if I looked at it from a certain angle. On a bad shift, I'd spend maybe twenty minutes out of eight hours dealing with people buying stems. On a good day, maybe a minute or two, tops. But the moments were there, and being complicit in them was a moral conundrum that I wrestled with a lot and never resolved.

Ultimately, the real reason I stayed was simple: It was about fear. Little has ever scared me more than being unemployed, the yawning maw of joblessness, the vulnerability of it. Because of how scary looking for work felt, how incapable of throwing myself into the application process I was, how poorly I fared in interviews, once I got a job, I held on to it for all I was worth. I had stayed too long at all my past jobs, had only ever been fired once my motivation sagged and my body gave out from under me. I'd never been able to call it, never been able to say, "I quit." This place was no different. When you feel like you're drowning, what do you care about the morals of the company that manufactured the life preserver?

/

Jimmy wasn't the only unhoused person I got to know while working at the corner store. I don't remember when I first met Russell; he'd been a regular for a long time before he really entered my consciousness. I knew him as an older Black man who wore a Manchester United ball cap and bought newspapers from time to time, typically the higher-end ones, but never seemed interested in chatting with me.

Then one day he came in and started talking. He'd gotten a letter in his PO box—this is when he told me he no longer had an apartment—stating that he owed more than $5,000 to his credit card company. His teacher's pension was barely enough to live off, he said. There was no way he'd be able to pay back the money. I asked where the debt had come from. "Well," he told me, "I knew that I owed it. But after a while they stopped contacting me about it."

It wasn't unusual for regulars to tell me about their problems. But it was rare for someone who'd previously not had much to say to suddenly become loquacious. After that first conversation, though, Russell decided that in me, he had someone who would listen. And evidently, he was at a point in his life where he needed someone to listen.

Over the next few months, Russell became a fixture at the store. He would show up in the evenings and stay until just before closing time at eleven. He would fall asleep in the dark-green wicker chair at the back of the store, by the little stand for filling out lottery slips, a collection of plastic bags bulging with newspapers at his feet. Increasingly, he felt less like a customer and more like an old man I had to babysit. He would ask me to set aside copies of newspapers, would barter to get a chocolate bar on credit. He would stand at my counter and talk to me for hours at a time, telling me about his life, his troubles, his successes and failures, a barely edited stream-of-consciousness ramble. Coming from any of the other regulars, all these behaviours would have been infuriating, but with Russell, it was different.

His story came to me in pieces. The big details settled in early. He was from the American South, had experienced the civil rights movement first-hand, had gone to a historically Black college, had dodged the draft, had moved to Montreal for his master's degree, then had taught history at nearby Dawson College for a decade plus. Now, he was homeless, an alcoholic, and in the early stages of Alzheimer's.

The rest—the detailing, the shading that filled him out—came in brief, illuminating glimpses. He loved to brag: about the white woman twenty years his senior he'd seduced while marching as a twentysomething; about the neo-Nazis he'd taken a baseball bat to in the eighties in Montreal; about the myriad bars he'd been kicked out of for being too good at pool; about the psychopathic murderer he'd taught an English course to at a prison; about the scarf from a young female admirer he'd worn during the student strikes wrapped around his neck like a keffiyeh.

In order to retain a degree of control, I insisted on treating him like a child. I told him when I couldn't talk, when I needed him to leave, that he had to get out of the chair. In some of these dicta, I was just repeating what my bosses had told me, but in some of them I was playing the heavy, insistent that my words had some weight to them. He was good-natured about it, considering I was a sheltered white kid with all the life experience he had in his pinky finger. I'm not sure what exactly he thought of me, though one day he told me I should be a teacher. I was smart, he said, and I had opinions. Considering who it was coming from, to this day, it's one of the nicest compliments I've ever been paid.

/

For many of the people I sold stems to, I got the sense it was something they had practically been born into. Sometimes they would come into the store with their relatives—a grown woman and her mother, or two cousins. One time a First Nations woman came in with her daughter, a toddler, and as she was paying for her stem a man walked in. He turned out to be the girl's father, and the three of them had a tragic, crack-tainted family reunion in front of my counter. Moments like that made me wonder why I didn't refuse to sell them the pipes, sometimes. I would wonder it as I swung open the cupboard behind the counter, would wonder it as I took their money and punched *$5.00* into the cash, would wonder it as they walked out the door.

Many of the things I experienced at the store happened at a bit of a remove for me. As a university student, I was only at this job temporarily. My parents were paying the rent on my shoebox apartment; my incredibly cheap in-province Quebec tuition was covered by money they'd set aside when I was growing up. I was here scrabbling together a few hundred bucks a month to pay for food and internet and a cellphone while I invested the bulk of my time into becoming a writer, taking creative writing classes and editing for the school paper. I could not imagine what it was like to lead these lives, which seemed so circumscribed by poverty, drugs, pain, chasing the same too-short high over and over and over again. Sometimes they would come to the store drunk, high, combative. Sometimes they'd disappear—I wouldn't see a regular for a shift or two but wouldn't realize they'd been missing until weeks had gone by.

I remember inquiring after one of them—Eric, a small Inuit man who would shoplift cases of Red Bull out at the giant supermarkets in the suburbs and come downtown to sell them—with Noah, a friend of his.

"He's in prison, man," Noah said.

/

Of course, things with Russell weren't all rosy. Outside the doors of the store, he was struggling, and those struggles managed to follow his stories when he entered. One night, drunk, standing by my counter, he shit his pants.

Realizing that a grown man you know by name has shit his pants in front of you—when what you thought was a bad fart just doesn't go away but worsens—felt like another level. He asked to use the washroom, but it wasn't for customers. I could have made an exception for him this one time, could have locked up the way I did for my own trips to the basement, but a wave of disgust rose up in me and I told him no. I told him to go somewhere else, and he went a few doors down, to a bakery/café owned by a friend of the brothers. The bakery owner came over later and told me Russell was barred from his place for life.

Why wasn't I kinder to him? A week or two later I called 411 for the first time and got them to patch me through to the Y so I could book a room for him at his request. He was the only customer I would have bothered to do something like that for; I knew that I owed him. He got me started reading Didion years before most of my peers when he pressed a copy of *Salvador* into my hands and assured me of its brilliance. An awful part of me had been tempted to keep it, to see if he'd remember having loaned it to me in the first place. I didn't, but the desire was symptomatic of my attempts to use his kindness to my advantage, certain that his presence in my life was valuable somehow, but incapable of seeing him simply as a friend—because he was a customer, because he was in his late sixties, because he was homeless.

I settled on wanting to write about him. He told me other people had done profile pieces on him, that there'd been one by Louis Rastelli for his *Fish Piss* zine and one on the Dawson College website, and I found them both online. I started bringing my phone out surreptitiously when he came in, and recording his tales. Somehow, I suppose because his best material kept me too spellbound to remember to record it, all I ended up with was an hour or two of barely intelligible, drunken meanderings. He'd weave details—about women he knew, his desire to write an op-ed about racial profiling, books he'd misplaced, tax documents, a trip to Mexico in his youth, fellow professors he was friends with, and his thoughts about the *printemps érable*—into a soliloquy about being barred from bars for hustling people at the pool table. I thought about asking him for a sit-down interview, even talked to a local online publication that expressed interest in publishing one, but it seemed crass. He was fading.

One night a woman came in and introduced herself as his daughter. She told me he'd had a heart attack and was in a rehabilitation centre on Sherbrooke Street. I asked her if she had his contact info, and she gave me the phone number of the centre and told me how to ask for him. A few days later I called and told him I'd like to stop by and chat Sunday evening, and would he mind? He said it'd be nice.

But when the day came I couldn't bring myself to go, too terrified at the thought of asking an alcoholism-rehabbing heart-attack survivor with Alzheimer's if he would let me use him for a story, and too caught up in my self-perception as a writer to consider going just for the sake of talking to him, of offering him some comfort.

I did see him on the street at least once or twice afterward, but skirted him, doing my best not to be seen. Afraid of reckoning with the way I'd treated him.

/

In January 2013, I missed a Saturday morning open shift, hungover from a party the night before. By the time I was out of bed, one of my fellow employees had been called in. The next day, I got a text from a co-worker asking me if I'd quit. The grumpy brother had told him that I had. I called the other brother, the friendly one, to talk. It only lasted about five minutes. He pointed out that I'd said recently I felt like I wasn't going to stick around. "Maybe this is just your way of quitting," he told me. It was nice of him—convincing me my firing had actually been my own decision. I told him to give me a call if he ever needed anyone for an emergency shift, but he never did, and I wasn't in a mood to fight for the job. I had some money in the bank as a result of some tidy tax returns, a windfall from my Ama's will, and a writing award I'd won at Concordia the winter before that I'd squirrelled away. I had pushed myself to stick with it for as long as I could. By now, I was just done with the job.

The store changed a lot about me over the course of the time I worked there—how much I knew about drugs, how comfortable I felt around matches and lighters and knives, how good I was at bargaining, how at ease I felt stealing things from my own workplace, how disposed I felt to give my spare change to panhandlers, how many people in the neighbourhood I knew by name—but it didn't change everything about me. One night a few months after I stopped working there, coming back home from a late-night grocery run, I noticed a tall man in a short-sleeved button-up playfully running his fingers along the bars in the store's windows before turning up the side street, probably a little drunk and carefree. But when I rounded the corner, the man hadn't meandered up the street; there he was, standing in the entranceway to the store.

It was my old boss, the angry, dark-haired one. He was cupping his hands to his mouth, and his lighter illuminated his face for a second. His eyes on his cigarette, he missed me. I had my headphones in; I was listening to the latest the National album, which seemed tailor-made for nighttime walks. I kept going, and I didn't hear him make a sound. I wondered for a second whether he'd seen me, whether he would have recognized me in the dark, how he felt about me. I imagined a conversation between us in my head. "We're very different, you and I," I imagined myself saying to him.

By now, I'd started worrying about my finances. I was about to graduate, still jobless and with no leads, but I realized then, in the last couple of steps back to my apartment, that I wouldn't trade places with him. He had money, but he wasn't free like I was. I didn't know where I was going to be a year from then. I didn't even know where I was going to be a month from then.

But he had a wife and three kids and a house, and the business he co-owned with his brother was only a few blocks away. He was tied down in those blocks, like a dog whose leash extends only so far. He wasn't going anywhere. He would be there, lighting up a cigarette late at night, selling porn mags, crack pipes, and lottery tickets to the city's saddest people, on that shitty, hopeless corner for years and years and years to come. Cornered, incarcerated, almost. There really was something to those bars on the windows.

It is being in Banff and going to the men's changing room at the hot springs. The little meltdown I have, the stress panic, when my lock won't work right and then I'm trapped, in my bathing suit, alone, the other writers steeping in the water outside, and me feeling so naked in bright lights and the maleness of the space. Until another writer, a male writer, came back and asked if I was okay. And I wasn't, needed his help to navigate it all. Brain shut down. Only coming back to myself in the hot water. Among the ungendered crowd. Unable to tell the other writers what happened.

Jaybird

When my mother first moved to Japan, she tried to jaywalk while pushing a stroller on an empty residential street. She was immediately stopped by an old, well dressed Japanese man who solemnly told her in perfect English "the downfall of society begins with the individual"
—@lillybilly299, Twitter

I cannot explain why but jaywalking with strangers makes me feel like I'm a part of something bigger than myself
—@divinely_x, Twitter

AS SOMEONE WHO GREW UP in the church and considered themself a devout Christian for much of my youth, rule-breaking was never a big part of my life.

Growing up, I was honest to a fault, couldn't stomach stealing or cheating, was almost never mean on purpose, felty guilty every time I masturbated, never skipped a single class in high school, had but a few sips from a single can of beer before I was comfortably in my twenties, didn't smoke weed until around the same time, and still haven't smoked a cigarette to this day. There've only ever been two things I felt comfortable doing even though I knew they were wrong: internet piracy, and jaywalking.

I'm one of those weird dinosaurs who never signed up for Spotify or even Apple Music, still carrying around actual song files on my digital devices like I'm stuck in 2012, but while there's probably a story to tell when it comes to my relationship to the long-suffering MP3, of the two vices, jaywalking is the one that inspires the most poetry in me.

It's not a new phenomenon, either. Like many other millennials, in the mid-2010s, when I was experimenting with the concept of a "personal brand" and looking for sentences to plug into my "bio" on digital platforms like

Facebook and Tinder, I reached for a phrase that I felt showed me in a fun, whimsical light to add to other ones like "hockey addict" and "pun wizard": "jaywalking all-star." In the span of two words, a gerund and a hyphenated compound, it encapsulated something of who I was: silly, creative, self-confident in a kind of slant way, and badass only within very tame constraints.

It was also, frankly, not dishonest. To whatever extent it's possible to be good at something no one else cares about, I'm really good at jaywalking. I'm not aware of any attempts to formalize or concretize the practice, but jaywalking well is something that requires skill, and it was then and is now something I do frequently, at times with the mundaneness of crossing any distance anywhere by placing one foot in front of the other, and at other times with a little heart-quickening rush, like I'm pulling off a very low-stakes heist. A victimless crime, a way of taking something back from the myriad forces that constrain free human movement in the urban milieu, a means of getting where one is going a little faster, and possibly with a slight tinge of verve.

What can I say? I grew up in downtown Montreal, a place with an off-kilter, artsy, bohemian vibe. Jaywalking was part of the tapestry of my life. But despite the fact that it was something I'd been practicing, consciously or otherwise, since childhood, along with the adjacent practice known to generations of Canadian kids as street hockey, I didn't start seriously thinking about jaywalking until about a decade ago, when I first tried to write an essay about it.

It was, generously, a mixed bag. It included a Douglas Adams witticism, a reference to a Hannibal Buress stand-up set, half a dozen intolerably corny bits of forced wordplay, and the phrase *the pig power structure*. It was in very bad need of an editor. At one point I wrote, "The same way graffiti and street art are the only kinds of art that matter anymore, imbued, by virtue of their illegality, with a special semantic *je ne sais quoi*, an illicit thrill, the knowledge that someone had the audacity to risk it all just to say something, jaywalking is an investment in the urban space that actually means something."

Despite the fact that I'm the kind of person in whose brain overly self-confident, nearly confrontational sentences like these occur quite frequently, in part because I'm someone who doesn't relish actual confrontation, and in part because I thus seek out friendships with people who don't come to it easily, I don't get into a lot of serious arguments with my friends. I reserve my provocative thoughts for safer spaces, like deleted email drafts, the inside of my skull, or books published by independent Canadian presses.

In 2018, though, I did get into an argument that I remember all too well, its emotional heft in direct inverse proportion to how long it lasted. Despite its brevity and lack of immediate consequences, it was one that functioned as a sort of omen, foreshadowing a schism six months later that would loom large over the whole of my life for years and years to come, one leak bursting in a dam in advance of the watershed moment.

The conversation that birthed the moment I remember took place in Banff, Alberta, a sort of mecca for Canadian artists of all stripes thanks to the presence of the Banff Centre for Arts and Creativity's year-round slate of workshops. I was visiting the city in order to work on a poetry collection about heartbreak and God that has still not seen the light of day.

So it was that, between bouts of writing and bouts of avoiding writing, while walking down from the Centre into town with two other members of my cohort, crossing the snow-covered street, I found myself in an argument about jaywalking.

/

Just as streets were invented and highways were invented and cars were invented and stoplights were invented, jaywalking had to be invented too; despite the primal feeling it can give off, it did not always exist. But while you can argue that the other items on that list were invented for good, in the name of progress, by humanity itself, jaywalking was invented by a very specific group of people for a very specific reason. It was invented by the automobile lobby, to make it easier for them to sell cars.

In fact, originally, *jaywalking* didn't mean crossing the street the wrong way, or illegally—it was a sidewalk-oriented version of jay-driving, when people (presumably country hicks) would drive on the wrong side of a road, not realizing the right side was the right side. This term came to be adopted for people committing similar—though perhaps less binaristic—faux pas on sidewalks, and this word was the one the automobile lobby reached for when it needed a scapegoat. In the 1910s, carmakers had run into an unpleasant reality about the experience of owning a car in early twentieth-century America: Pesky human beings had an awful habit of popping up right where they shouldn't be, in front of their customers' automobiles. *Ow—your face got in the way of my fist.*

In order to make sure the annoying experience of running someone over wasn't cutting into their bottom line, they had to devise a way for human beings to cede the roadways—a non-trivial portion of urban space that had long been shared between people and slower-moving carriages—to cars. But how to achieve such a goal, to reframe centuries-old human behaviour in short order before people rejected cars as being too likely to produce accidents? Luckily for them, mass media existed by then, and the auto lobby played it like a fiddle. Car manufacturers pooled their resources to create the journalistic arm of their lobbying efforts, a "news bureau" whose sole function was to send newspapers ready-made clippings that framed accidents where cars ran over people as the fault of the victim. Newspapers nationwide that needed some extra column inches could make use of this professionally typed yellow journalism at no cost.

One needn't be a scholar of history nor an understander of the effect that Fox News has had on America in recent decades to know what happened next: The tide of public sentiment turned against these bumbling jaywalkers. What were they doing in the street like that anyway, if they didn't want to be run over? Lawmakers hurried to attend to this pressing need—every day, it seemed, more stories about people being run over. Didn't they know the danger? Laws were put in place banning the practice. Just like that, the roads belonged to cars only. *À qui la rue? À eux, la rue.*

/

I stole that last line from the streets. When I was younger, in my mid-twenties, out walking late at night with friends, a few times I ambled out into the centre of the street, spread my arms wide, wingspan open to an imaginary audience, an imaginary coliseum, Russell Crowe in *Gladiator*, and shouted, "À qui la rue? À nous la rue!"

Whose street? Our street! And not just this one, this one that our feet are pressed against right now, but all of them—but the idea of there even being a street. Whose streets? Our streets. The ones that grid out the city we live in, the blocks we walk.

"À qui la rue? À nous la rue!" is one of the many chants that were employed by the people during the student movement in 2012, when Quebecers banded together, arm in arm, marching in the streets they owned—the streets their taxes had paid for and the streets their taxes would pay for forevermore, those Montreal streets, slapdash with asphalt, so famous for being riddled with potholes—banging pots and pans, making themselves heard until nothing could be heard but them, until through the din the provincial government realized tuition hikes were a non-starter.

When I was saying it aloud to those snowy midnight streets a decade ago, it was a joke, of course—at its peak, the red square movement had 300,000 out in the streets of downtown Montreal, and I was just a skinny kid in a dark toque and a black jacket. (If someone goes against a red light at night when there's no one around to see it, is it really breaking the law? Or is it, as the track "Yo Yeah" on the Mos Def and Talib Kweli collaboration *Black Star* has it, a form of brainwashing *not* to?)

But there's something there, still. Regardless of the disparity in our numbers, the *printemps érable* protestors had been doing as I was doing—pedestrians reclaiming the street, a space that is visibly and categorically not ours during the day—and my joking reappropriation of the chant, I realize, doubled as an homage to its power. Try it sometime, in winter, if you can, with a fresh coat of snow on the ground, ideally. Alone in the middle of the street, with no cars to fear and silence reigning, it really does feel like your street.

/

Part of what I love about jaywalking is that I love walking itself too much to let it be so boxed in by petty bourgeois constraints like municipal bylaws.

As someone who has lived their whole life in a place that people now might call a fifteen-minute city, and who still has never learned how to drive, walking has crossed over from being a mode of transportation into the territory of being a load-bearing part of my self-conception. I've loved walking places for as long as I can remember, figuring out the best routes to take, forming my own desire paths, cutting Pythagorean diagonals through the Cartesian grid of reality, my footprints little dotted lines stretching out behind me. Though biking is more economical, and public transit can do a wonderful job at protecting you from the elements, walking feels like the most honest form of movement I have.

It's also one that can be hard to talk about, given how little the average person seems to think about it. I once bonded with someone over our shared preference for walking long distances in new cities rather than trying to learn the local public transit system. Worse yet, I once wrote a treatise on how to do it well ("The Beginner's Footbook to Extreme Powerwalking"), trying to distill all the lessons I'd learned about using my feet to move from Point A to Point B, over 2,500 words of walking advice meted out across nine points, extolling the values of things like diagonals and fulcrums. Point 5 on the list was titled "Ignore the Stoplight." I'm not sure who such a text would be for, other than a younger version of me. But I think about it sometimes and laugh, laugh at how terribly neurodivergent it feels, how silly it is to care this much about something so, well, pedestrian.

That's not the only connection I see to the way my brain works. Most of the ADHD symptoms I experience could be better classified as just plain ADD. Hyperactivity has never really been part of my arsenal. I'm great at using my laptop to avoid a task. Great at using my phone to avoid a task. Great at using excuses to avoid a task, a serial liar fooling my naive self over and over and over about when something will be done, when I'll arrive someplace. A thousand late assignments, missed opportunities, myriad failures, and various points along the spectrum of underwhelm. Why can't I just get it done earlier? Why can't I be better at this? Why does every other thing in the world have a more solid claim on my attention right now? ADHD nothing so much as a means of feeling bad about myself. My body is a machine that turns assigned tasks into shame.

But the closest I have to the *H* of hyperactivity is probably the antsiness I get at red lights and stop signs. The get-up-and-go, the scanning—for oncoming traffic, crossing pedestrians, cops within eyesight. Waiting for the moment. A habit I associated, from living in a poor part of downtown for six years, with people I recognized as drug users. The fix more important than traffic. Or the social contract. Was I much different? Besides nicer clothes, and the recency of a shower and shave. A voice in my head telling me it was okay. To cross if I wanted to.

In my case there's rarely even anything important on the other side of the road. Sometimes (often) it's because I'm running late, but just as often it's the feeling of not having to wait anymore, the feeling of having broken through stasis and into the freedom of movement again. Like a spent jerk-off, whenever I get to the other side, a flicker of guilt goes through me. What was wrong with me? I wondered. Why couldn't I just stand there? Post-nut clarity. The pent-up desire that forced me onto the road a few metres back now gone. I slow, start to take in my surroundings. What if that had been a cop car? What if those children saw? What will they think? I explain myself to their furious parents in lengthy internal monologue. The rule of law doesn't define that's right—what's right defines the rule of law, but imperfectly. There are gaps, fissures, cracks, where the wrong gets in. I mean, jaywalking isn't hurting anyone. Eventually—perhaps at the next set of lights—I'm distracted from my silent defences.

/

Here's what I remember about the argument over jaywalking I got into in Banff in 2018: I remember an old friend, a new friend, and I—three members of the Winter Writers Retreat cohort that January—walking, in the middle of the road, down into (or up back from) the town of Banff itself. Me, moved to share, extolling to the two of them (women) the virtues of jaywalking, of taking back what had been taken from us. Public space. The way every city is now a space for cars first and people a distant second. My friend turning to (on) me. "That's such a man thing to say. You're just mad because there's one place you're not allowed to go." Me, gobsmacked. Not yet out as non-binary. To myself or her or anyone. Just knowing I didn't want to be a man, didn't feel like one, and didn't understand her now throwing this conception of me in my face. Thinking we were all on the same side, now feeling attacked. Protesting half-heartedly. Trying to explain that losing the commons to capitalist car culture was not a gender issue. That we were all worse off for it. Stumbling. Giving it up. Letting the snowfall have its say instead.

And I did, and I do, benefit from male privilege. And I was assigned, raised, socialized male. And I have, in recent years, paid more attention to who jaywalks. Or especially jay-bikes. How frequently it's guys. Impulsive. Impatient. Selfish. Crossing on red while women wait. Law-abiding. Safe. Non-confrontational. How jaywalking, in places where it's illegal, speaks of a kind of privilege: I'm not that afraid of the cops. I can afford to be hit by a fine. The opinions of passersby don't really matter to me.

So maybe it is a very masculine perspective to say it's good to jaywalk. But is that wrong of me? To want to reclaim the space that has been taken from us by the automobile industry. The metal boxes that have remade our cities in their image. That have trapped the planet in smog. So many hours lost to traffic. So many lives lost to crashes. Our conception of what anything could look like sanded down by the auto industry lobby. Everything else collateral damage. The ease of use of the car experience always prioritized over the hiccuping, disjointed public transit: seeing, hearing, smelling—being among strangers. Waiting for a bus or a train. Walking the extra few blocks from your stop. In the rain, the snow, the cold, the wind, the cruel summer sun. All things obviated by the ability to drive up to your front door, park in the driveway, the garage, back to the smiling wife, the 2.5 kids.

Like cigarettes, I know I have an extreme position on cars. I'll admit grudgingly that they have some positive points. Think of all the lives that have been saved when someone's been rushed to hospital without needing an ambulance to arrive first. Think of all the back seat makeouts that have led to love, to marriage, to children. Think of all the meandering drives to nowhere that helped someone untangle a problem knotted up in their brains. All the secrets opened up and admitted to between family members on quiet back-country roads, each staring ahead, not having to avert their gazes from the sheer intimacy of the moment. *Son, it's about time you knew. Mom, I can't keep lying about this. Oh, honey.*

But what about the moments that have been stolen from us by the complete dependence on cars? What of all the friendships never formed because two people each drove to the same place rather than sitting next to each other on a train there? The love stories that might have blossomed between two people who were cut down, in the prime of their lives, in accidents? The generations of humans living in harmony in a timeline where carbon emissions never threatened the balance of our ecosystems? What of the timeline where my younger sister was never side-swiped by a car coming home one night, never had to be hospitalized?

/

In 2024, jaywalking was decriminalized in New York City. The cops had been using jaywalking's illegality as a pretext to indiscriminately stop Black and brown people, and now they wouldn't be able to—or rather, now it would be slightly more difficult for them to racially profile and harass people of colour. As the bill's sponsor, council member Mercedes Narcisse of Brooklyn, told NPR, "Let's be real: jaywalking is a way of life in New York City. It's how people navigate our city."[21]

What is really being said is that *walking* is a way of life. As it has been for millennia, since before there were humans, since before there were bipeds. One of the things I do every day that connects me to my ancestors, to all the people who combined to produce me. How short, how brief, how insignificant the era of the car by comparison.

In any case. If I die in a car crash, as pedestrians and cyclists (and people in cars) so often do in cities designed against them, it'll be easy to look back at what I've written here and say that I had it coming. There are lots of things I wouldn't be caught dead doing, not in the literal sense, but if I die jaywalking, before Montreal has the good sense to decriminalize it as well, you can at least say I died doing something I loved.

21 Alana Wise, "Enforcement Was Considered Discriminatory. Now New Yorkers Can Jaywalk Legally," NPR, October 30, 2024, https://www.npr.org/2024/10/30/nx-s1-5172504/jaywalking-legal-new-york-city.

It is a history of wanting to remove myself from things. Wanting to be neutral, nothing, not. Not associated with a long legacy of hurt, of cruelty, of domination. Not acting in a context of harm. Did I ever have queer ancestors? Pale and ashamed of themselves somewhere in the British Isles. It is the little ways that my body and my ingrained habits felt more feminine than masculine. The way I'd always peed sitting down unless there were urinals. The way I'd jerked off for so long, rotating my thumb around the head, no attention paid to the shaft. Like I was playing with a clitoris. That had just been what felt natural to me when I first started. A surprise to learn in ninth grade the others did it differently. From a gesture. In enriched biology.

Mourning Drunk

IT'S AN UNACKNOWLEDGED TRUISM that song lyrics are supposed to rhyme, one of those rules of the form that you may not even really realize is a rule until you see it being broken. That an ending line, in possession of a syllable, must be in want of a rhyme. The way a rhyme is an opening and its close, a debt and its repayment. A question and its answer, a promise and its fulfillment. The way *birth* rhymes with *death*, the unrhymed line a hanging emptiness.

I think about these things in a church, at a choral performance. A young non-binary person singing "early music," haunting, formless religious syllables from before the rhyme was invented.

While rocking back and forth between the basic ABCB and the slightly frillier ABAB rhyme schemes that dominate so much of pop music is pleasing enough, I also find myself drawn to the far ends of the spectrum that the two exist on: all the way from someone like MF DOOM, a rapper who constructed verses out of four- and five- and six-syllable rhymes with shocking regularity, to a band like Michigan post-hardcore outfit La Dispute.

Fronted by Jordan Dreyer, La Dispute has released five albums of music, all hewing to a fascinating sonic principle: What if an angry punk song's vocals didn't have to be sung or screamed and didn't have to rhyme, but were instead more akin to short stories or diary entries, free-form and focused more on narrative and feeling than on sound?

In the summer of 2009, I found myself taken with their breakup-focused debut full-length, *Somewhere at the Bottom of the River Between Vega and Altair,* released the year prior. But their 2011 follow-up, *Wildlife,* which felt more mature, its topics broader in scope, produced two of the most haunting songs I've ever heard: "Edward Benz, 27 Times" (which describes a stabbing) and "King Park" (which describes a presumed gang shooting).

Both stories are told in the past tense, but where "Edward Benz" explores what happened in a matter-of-fact way that belies its grim subject matter, "King Park" plays an interesting trick—we find the narrator excorporating himself in order to experience the crime, a metaphysical version of CSI or *Law & Order,* becoming a camera of sorts. (It's hard to imagine shouting along with lines like that in a rowdy mosh pit, but Dreyer's earnest delivery makes his material work.)

> *Shots were fired from an SUV heading northbound, Eastown*
> *The target a rival—but they didn't hit the target this time*
> *They hit a kid we think had nothing to do with it*
> *And I travel backwards through time and space and*
> *I disintegrate, become invisible*
> *I wanna see it where I couldn't when it happened*
> *I wanna see it all first hand this time*
> *I want to know what it felt like*

I get it. I used to feel that way about death, too.

/

So many people drink when they're sad, but the prosaic kinds of drunkenness most of us tend to trade in—vague malaise drunk, or unrequited feelings drunk, or shitty workweek drunk—are orders of magnitude kinder than mourning drunk. Mourning drunk is a feeling unique in both scope and tenor. It's analogous, in some sense, to pinching your own arm when you have a headache; you're using a litany of smaller, sharper, localized pains to distract your brain from the dull, overarching, insurmountable pain.

The first time I got mourning drunk was a cloudy day in August many summers ago. I was with Melissa and Marie. Melissa, my best friend, was home from Brooklyn, where she was working in a hospital, fixing poor kids' teeth. Marie, the ex I'd lost my virginity to, was a tall school friend of ours with a brain the size of a planet. The occasion was that Marie's mother had just succumbed to cancer, a condition when something goes wrong and the body attacks itself, causing death.

None of us were ever particularly responsible drinkers in the first half of our twenties, but mourning-drunk us was something else. As day bled into night, we talked about everything and anything but the fresh death hovering over Marie, trying, roughly, to drink ourselves into the ground, or at least to dismantle whatever it was that was keeping us from falling over. The venomous undercurrent. Saying "fuck you" to life.

Here's how we did it: Around 5 p.m. the three of us walked into a boring little place in Montreal's sleepy Notre-Dame-de-Grâce neighbourhood. The place was called the NextDoor Pub. The first song they played was "Bang Bang (My Baby Shot Me Down)" and the second was "Stand by Me" and then they played "Let's Get It On" not too long after. Whoever constructed the playlist, employee or algorithm, must have known we were in our feelings. By the time we left about two hours later, I'd had an amaretto sour, a double Maker's Mark on the rocks, and one third of the twenty-four picklebacks our friendly server had brought us.

If you've never had a pickleback before, good on you. A pickleback is an extremely concentrated form of self-destruction. It works like this: You take one shot of Jameson and immediately chase it with one shot of pickle juice. Melissa had just moved to Brooklyn a few months earlier and picklebacks were the hot new thing there at the time, she explained, so we felt like we were trendsetters, in a way. We had to explain the concept to our server at first, but they had pickle juice on hand, so who knows, maybe we weren't the first people to order picklebacks at the NextDoor Pub.

The thing about the pickle juice is that it's so strong it erases the whiskey completely, without leaving any trace of its own passage; in essence, a pickleback is a tricky, ersatz time machine that brings you back to the moment right before you did the shot. Your mouth doesn't remember what happened, but your body still has the alcohol inside it. If you've seen enough time travel movies, you know that the more you take advantage of a loophole in physics like that, the riskier it gets. The body starts to break down. Who knows what might happen to your cells.

We didn't give a damn, though. We just kept ordering them, freshly addicted, delighted by the strangeness, the surprise burst of the disappearing alcohol, the way the two flavours perfectly cancelled each other out. Like chasing an acid with a base. Inhale, exhale. We'd finish a round and ask for the next one, ready to go back in time again, pickle juice still fresh on our breath. We never were able to go far enough back to when Marie's mom was still alive, but after a few rounds, maybe that wasn't even the point anymore.

When the bill finally came, it read $139.25. I had privately decided about twenty minutes earlier that I was going to grab the whole thing because, I reasoned, you shouldn't have to pay to get drunk on the occasion of your mother just died, and I wasn't confident in my ability to navigate the conversation should it arise. Instead, I pulled a power move. When our server came, I said, "One bill," jabbing a single finger up in the air with the self-assuredness of a version of myself much richer than I actually was at the time. A future self, with a future paycheque.

It took me three tries with the credit card machine, but I was finally able to get the total to read an even $200, and then the final round of picklebacks was on our server, and everyone laughed and felt friendly and exchanged names. My name was Alex. My friends were Marie and Melissa. The server's name was Danielle. She smiled at me as we walked out, in what must have been an embarrassed way, although it did make me feel incredibly handsome.

/

As the guitars and drums behind him grow increasingly urgent, Dreyer walks us up to the rhymeless precipice of "King Park," a motel standoff between the shooter and police waiting outside the room, knowing he's inside and armed.

I floated up through the window of a room to the west
I hovered out to the hallway, tried to listen in
I heard them trying to reason, get him to open the door
His uncle begging and pleading, half-collapsed to the floor
He preached of hope and forgiveness
Said, "There is always a chance to rectify what you've taken
Make your peace in the world"

I wonder if old people think about making peace. Knowing, statistically, that they're closer to death than birth. I hadn't known Marie's mom well.

I recall her as flashes of feelings—a green wallpaper bordering on turquoise, and the sensation of a presence padding around a cozy west-end apartment while Marie and I lay in bed together, teenagers curled into a set of punctuation marks on a twin-size. I remembered a photo of the pope, and a crucifix over a doorway, though Marie later clarified these were more to placate her Polish grandmother than a sign of her mother's deep religious devotion.

She had always been nice to me. I sensed that she'd appreciated that her profoundly unique daughter had in me first a romantic interest and later, perhaps, the sort of friend who'd come visit her in the hospital when her mother was slipping away.

/

After we left the pub, the three of us bought cones at a gourmet ice cream place nearby and then took a cab to another, fancier bar. But that bar was full to bursting, so we took another cab to another, yet fancier bar that wasn't, and split a bottle of sake there.

The final bar had four sake options—a Japanese one at $20, an American one at $40, a Japanese one at $60, and a Japanese one at $115. I did a bit of mental math and settled on the $60 one, but realistically, by then we were too drunk to know the difference between good sake and bad sake. Before we'd settled on the bottle, Melissa actually asked them if they served picklebacks. But it wasn't that kind of place.

After we finished the $60 bottle we left the sake bar, and the three of us went to the nearest liquor store. Deep under the spell of the mourning drunk, I anted up and bought a bottle of Grey Goose. I'd always wanted to buy a bottle of Grey Goose, ever since I'd had a glass in an airport bar a few days before Christmas in 2009 after saying goodbye to the girl I was dating at the time, who was flying to Paris for Christmas to stay with her grandparents.

Her father had driven us to the airport and then, after she'd snaked her way down the international departures line, he had offered to buy me whatever I wanted at the airport bar. I decided I wanted something I'd never had before and requested a Grey Goose. When asked if I wanted it "on the rocks" I said yes, although I didn't know what that meant at the time; I just liked the way it sounded, like I was a crashing wave, a fine spray of sea mist.

Not long after I'd finished the glass I felt this incredible warmth spreading through my chest. All of a sudden I understood why Russians drank vodka.

If I'd walked through the X-ray machine then I bet they would have seen the fiery roots of it criss-crossing my torso in slow-mo.

While I was getting the bottle of Grey Goose, Melissa was buying a bottle of Mumm Napa rosé and a sixer of Palm Bay, though she immediately gave the whole thing of Palm Bay to a man who was begging outside of the liquor store. It was dark and raining and he was sitting cross-legged on the sidewalk. He seemed thankful, but then, maybe he didn't know what Palm Bay tasted like yet. "It's not a beer, it's a spritz," I told Melissa the next day, after googling Palm Bay to find out what exactly it was.

Then we went to the grocery store across the street and bought snacks. I bought Miss Vickie's chips. Marie bought a jar of dill pickles. When we got out, the guy had disappeared into the night, sixer of Palm Bay and all, although it was still raining.

/

Have you ever cracked open a can of Palm Bay? It's like the end of summer—it just happens. It slides by and there's nothing you can do about it but keep drinking. Drinking Palm Bay is a highly concentrated form of giving up. It's the Photoshop Gaussian blur filter set over the whole of your consciousness. It's jerking off on the couch at 5 p.m. and then taking a depression nap. It's sweatpants in a dark-blue can.

The first time I drank Palm Bay, I was hanging out at a party when the future ex-boyfriend of a future ex-friend of mine showed up with a sixer. They'd just started dating recently and it was either my first or second time meeting him. He was always very quiet, which was weird, because he was a rock star. His band had just been longlisted for the Polaris Music Prize, which made him the most successful person I'd ever been at a party with, I think. He stood there and nodded at people. I cracked a can and took a sip. Nothing happened. Which, I realized later, was the whole point of Palm Bay.

The second time I drank Palm Bay was at a springtime birthday party. It was the first party that me and my second-most-recent ex both went to after the breakup. We were on the back balcony with everyone else, pretending that everything was fine. That everything was chill. That everything was Palm Bay, easy breezy. The middle button on my ex's dress had come undone and I could see through to their stomach, a little hole in reality, a secret intimacy. I didn't say anything.

By the end of the night, the two of us ended up sitting outside together on the back balcony, the rest of the party having migrated indoors. Somehow, they were in my arms. By then it was completely dark out. I kissed them on the cheek and they turned to face me. One of their friends came out and saw us and went back inside. We were an embarrassing thing, an unsightly stain on the party. You're supposed to know better. That's Palm Bay for you.

/

After the liquor store, the three of us made our way back to my apartment, albeit with some difficulty. Melissa was the shortest of the three of us by about half a foot and wasted out of her mind, yelling things at passersby.

"Don't judge me," she yelled at a confused couple who had wandered by during her ramblings. "I'm actually a business professional!" I wondered whether her being a dentist made the behaviour more or less embarrassing.

Somehow, she ended up being the one carrying the Grey Goose, and she was wielding it like a manic wizard wields a sceptre in the climactic battle of a really bad movie. I was worried she was going to smash it on something and all the precious nostalgic clear alcoholic juice inside would disappear into the concrete in little invisible rivulets, like tears in rain.

When we got back to my place, we play-acted like we were going to keep the good times rolling. I got out a thing of hummus for the Miss Vickie's and we poured the rosé into glasses. I think, maybe, we were going to sit on my bed and watch a movie, but Melissa got up to go to the bathroom.

As I talked to Marie I absent-mindedly wondered why Melissa was brushing her teeth, because she kept on spitting toothpaste into the sink. That's honestly what it sounded like. But then Marie got up with a weary sense of purpose and went to the bathroom to hold Melissa's hair back, and that about signalled the end of the night.

After Melissa was done vomiting, I put them both in an Uber, and Marie pretended she was named Alex because it was 2014 and neither she nor Melissa had an Uber account yet. I waved goodbye to the disappearing car, nameless, hoping nothing would go wrong, hoping Marie knew how to act like an Alex.

It felt like we had lived a lifetime together, but when I got back in the apartment I realized it was somehow only 10 p.m.

/

Though I saw her one more time, slumbering, in the waning weeks, the last time I actually spoke with Marie's mother was the night she moved into the hospital full-time. She'd collapsed, and Marie had called an ambulance, and when they'd gotten to the hospital there were somehow no pillows for her mother, she explained on the phone.

So I brought a pillow, and a bag of yogurt-and-green-onion Kettle chips, and a book, and her mother laughed at me, because it was the best pillow I owned and it was still thinner and more ragged looking than any of the pillows they had at home, a Dickensian orphan pillow, a shadow of a real pillow.

That night, I slept over at Marie's place and, in the simultaneously giving and pragmatic spirit of her dying Polish mother, she sent me home the next morning with their worst pillow, to replace my own. It was an unqualified pillow upgrade. But it's strange to look back now and think about how I managed to disappoint a dying woman with the gift of a shitty pillow.

Working as I was at a website, our office's annual Spa Day was the next morning. I was in no shape to be at a spa, or on a beach, or on a boat with my co-workers, even accounting for all the free drinks. I texted to let them know I was sick and wouldn't make it, but I still ended up having to pay for the massage I'd scheduled at the spa.

The funny thing was, because the massage didn't actually take place, I had to pay out of pocket for the absence of a massage while my co-workers were reimbursed for the massages they did get by our health insurance policy. I still think about the irony of paying not to get a massage sometimes. But life is full of little absurdities, when you look close enough.

/

If *in medias res* is the John Milton–approved way to drop a reader into a story, Dreyer ends "King Park" *ex medias res,* one might say—a thorny hangnail of a theological question mixed with a Chekhov's gun, Nabokov's phone call–type Schrödinger's-cat scenario as the narrator hangs just outside the room and at last hears the shooter speak. It was an accident, he shouts, repeating, "*Can I still get into heaven if I kill myself?*" over and over, seeing this as a way to atone for his crime. Then, on a dime, much of the intensity drains out of the song as the lyrics switch back from the shooter's words to the narrator's: "*I left the hotel behind / Don't wanna know how it ends.*"

That last line comes back to me often. Why are we so obsessed with knowing how things end? *I left the hotel behind. Don't wanna know how it ends.* I've read that ideas are like viruses. The traditional beginning-middle-end story structure is a particularly contagious one.

/

We're all robbed of our loved ones before their time, I know. Spouses don't come home from work. Parents drop dead in the middle of the night, heart stopped, head smashed on the bathroom tiles. Younger siblings turn the wrong way in their cribs. I got lucky. Through some cosmic miracle of untold quadrillions of collectively combining trends, decisions, and coincidences, it wasn't until a few months before my twenty-fifth birthday that one of my relatives died.

Until then, death had mostly been weaving around the edges of my life, a perimeter player not yet ready to go to the dirty areas. My great-great-grandmother and an assortment of great-aunts and great-uncles had passed away here and there, distant black stars dotting the firmament of my childhood otherwise unsullied by tragedy, but no one with whom I had any kind of personal relationship died until my maternal grandmother, who I knew as Ama (and who always called me Sasha) but who was born Judith, succumbed to her own year-long bout with cancer.

Hers was in her throat, lodged there by the thousands and thousands of cigarettes she had leaned on for happiness through a lonely, unhappy life devoid of socializing, exploring, or loving. Pregnant with my aunt at the close of her teens, she had raised two children with an even younger husband, Dennis, who left her for another woman once their children moved out. Apart from a brief, ill-fated stint living with my acerbic aunt, she lived by herself for the rest of her life, until, I suppose, the final weeks in the hospital, working as a librarian, books—so it seemed to me—her whole world.

I was lucky, also, in that I got to say goodbye. I didn't approach that last conversation with the certainty of its finality—you always imagine there'll be more—but it was clear that the end was near. She had always been fragile—frail, skinny, and barely there, every hug held ever so slightly back by concern that I might hurt her—but by then she was skeletal, death showing through. I don't remember what we talked about, which feels like a missed opportunity to have said something of value, but I remember there being a feeling of understanding between us.

We had always been similar—shy, thin people with a lot of emotions and not enough friends, busying ourselves with the tidy simplicity of books and words to drown out the inscrutable complexities of real life—but I never really realized how much so until she first got the diagnosis. We saw each other more frequently that year, felt free to speak about more varied topics, found ourselves learning more about each other. We grew, in a word, closer. It wasn't a closeness hurriedly stitched together by the looming prospect of her death; it was more that the diagnosis served as a reminder: that our lives, and the people who populate them, are temporary.

A few days later, my mother told us she was gone. My sister and I didn't go to the funeral, which was several hours away and attended by just a handful of people. Over the course of that summer I wrote a few poems about her, like after I cashed the cheque from her will. The weird morbidity of that.

/

In a way, though, that night of drinking with Marie and Melissa was my first real taste of mourning. After Marie's mom's funeral, a group of us rode in cars to the cemetery for the burial. It was incredibly hot and sunny. It seemed ridiculous, somehow, that we were all wearing black, dressed to our respective nines, standing under the unrelenting brightness of it all.

The funeral men were burying Marie's mother in a part of the cemetery where the grass was patchy and yellow. It seemed more like a vacant lot. I wondered if that wasn't a little disappointing for Marie. Afterward, a group of us got a fancy lunch in a backyard *terrasse*, then went to see *Guardians of the Galaxy*, and then ended up at a bar downtown. I don't think we knew it when we got there, but we were destined to order a round of picklebacks about half an hour in, and after that, another round, like there was some force greater than us controlling our actions. The pickle juice they were using wasn't as good as the pickle juice at the NextDoor Pub had been, though. Something was off—the tang, or the dill mix, or whatever.

After that, we went out for Chinese, and after that, we went to a nice new tiki bar in a Chinatown basement. I'd gone there earlier in the summer with someone who'd stopped seeing me since, though a few years later we'd hook up again and then stop seeing each other again. Two of us split a drink that came in a coconut, and two of us split a drink that came in a pineapple.

I got up at the end and grabbed the tab. I knew it was the right thing to do, because the waiter didn't even ask me if I was paying for all four of us, he just rang it up like that.

/

The day after our trip to the liquor store, Marie told me that if she'd been sober she would have told me not to buy Grey Goose. "What should I have bought?" I asked her. "Belvedere. Or Chopin. Or Wyborowa. Or Żubrówka," she said.

It seemed like I was always making the wrong choices when it came to alcohol. Everything I chose was too girly or too pretentious or too cheap, exposing me as a booze rookie. I wondered if there was anything I could drink that I couldn't also feel embarrassed about. But maybe there's no drink that you can't feel embarrassed by or proud of drinking if you put the right spin on it.

At the end of the day, you're just trying to numb whatever pain it is that you're feeling. Do people who take painkillers judge each other for the different brands they use?

/

A few years after Ama passed away, I was in Old Montreal, fresh out of a trip to the boat spa there, when I found out my aunt Teresa had died. The bar Blair and I were en route to was called the Coldroom, which in retrospect feels morbid. What is death but a cold room, anyway? Like walk-in freezers, something you get trapped inside of.

My father had called a few times while my phone was in the spa locker, which I knew was probably a sign that something bad had happened. He's not much of an impromptu caller, and certainly not a double-caller. When I reached him, I found out that he'd already flown back from Europe, cutting a business trip short, but hadn't contacted me until he landed. He told me I should sit down. I started flitting through all the different family members it might have been—the older ones, the ones who weren't doing well, the ones who seemed likely to engage in reckless behaviour. I wasn't expecting to hear her name.

As we'd learn later, she had taken her own life. Suicide, a condition when something goes wrong and the body attacks itself, causing death. I was shocked. From my perspective, there'd been no warning signs. It's true that the last time I'd seen her, a few months prior, she'd unexpectedly left a family brunch early with her daughter and had seemed kind of distant. And her husband, my uncle Paul, driving me back from the brunch, had explained in the car that she hadn't been doing super well. But it's not something you expect. You always imagine there'll be more.

I sat down on a stoop on Rue Saint-Paul and listened to my dad talk for a bit. I promised to be there for the funeral the following weekend. She was maybe the member of my extended family I liked best, someone I'd want to talk to even if we weren't related, a vivacious woman with a can-do attitude and a propensity for laughter that none of my blood relatives could match. She had two kids, a husband, an English retriever named Tucker, a nice house in a suburb of Toronto. But. She was on medical leave from work and had been in a dark place for months, had been in treatment at a nearby hospital. Her family was worried she was a danger to herself.

The rest of us didn't find out until it was over.

By that point, Blair and I had run out of time to go to the Coldroom, so we skipped it and headed straight to Café Parvis, where we had post-spa dinner reservations. She'd said, "We can bail," but I told her I needed a bit of normalcy. Normalcy in the form of wood-fired oven pizza served on cutting board slabs instead of plates, and salads with a double-digit number of ingredients.

At the restaurant I drank two expensive Scotches, but it was more an attempt to unsober myself than an attempt at self-annihilation. I was still in the shock of it. I didn't want to destroy my consciousness, I just wanted to float in a warm bath a little bit. I didn't cry then, or at the funeral, where, dressed in a newly purchased dark-grey suit and a black turtleneck, I was one of the white-gloved pallbearers, though I did cry at the wake, flimsy plastic water bottle in hand, and again in Kampai Garden, another Montreal bar, a few months later, most of the way done a way-too-sweet cocktail, when we were talking about weddings with a friend of Blair's. I flashed back to a memory I'd had from the year before Teresa died, of imagining her smiling at me at my wedding one day, a past future that would now never come to pass. The deafening silence of the unrhymed line. Its awful emptiness.

To this day I don't know how she did it, who found her, any of that. It was a closed-casket funeral. My father's side of the family aren't big sharers. If you know and you're reading this, don't reach out to tell me, please. I left the hotel behind.

It is liking to talk to women instead of men. It is liking to talk to genderqueer people. Though always feeling not non-binary enough to really be non-binary. On the dating apps, seeing people who are so androgynous I can't tell. Being jealous. It is missing being young and skinny and hairless. Because that was what felt feminine and sleek and sexy to me. Though back then I didn't know how to dress or style or groom myself. Never shown by anyone. Too scared to explore. It is waxing my legs with my female roommates in 2007 or so. Little pop of gender euphoria. But not enough to have done it since. It is hating to shave, although this means I grow facial hair, because looking in the mirror while running a razor through it reminds me. An accusation in visual form. Man. Man. Man. Shaving once every six to eight weeks easier. Saving up for one long session in front of the sink. Then back to smooth.

Behind the Masc

WHATEVER PROGRESS ALONG THE MORAL ARC of the universe queer people have made, some spaces will always remain unfriendly to them. When defenceman Luke Prokop came out as gay in July 2021, by virtue of the fact that his rights were held by the Nashville Predators, he became the only out male player in hockey history to have a relationship with a professional team.

Prokop, of course, is not the first male pro athlete to come out as gay. A number of players in the rest of the big four North American sports leagues—basketball, football, and baseball—have done so, many after retiring. Michael Sam, an NFL prospect, came out before being drafted and ultimately never played a game in the league. In women's hockey, meanwhile, a number of star players have come out to virtually no controversy, and some have even married each other. Yet, in men's hockey, we have only Prokop. Midway through the third decade of the twenty-first century, no player who has come out as any stripe of queer has ever set foot on NHL ice.

Of course, if something like a public coming out has happened only a handful of times in the other team sports, it's hardly surprising to see it fail to appear in hockey. Zero, after all, is not a much smaller number than one or two.

But any hockey fan who's watched a 1–0 game is familiar with the vastness of that difference. It seems to me there's something about men's hockey—a sport about which comedian Rodney Dangerfield once reportedly quipped, "I went to a fight last night and a hockey game broke out"—that's especially unfriendly to queerness. Its core culture remains one of male aggression, where weakness of any kind, real or perceived, gets weaponized. I know what I'm talking about because I left hockey myself, largely over not being "manly enough."

Mainstream culture may have gotten more comfortable with homosexuality in recent decades, but hockey culture is not mainstream culture. Men's hockey has always been an old boys' club, an engine for reifying masculine physical sacrifice in the pursuit of glory, and an at times overt analog for the military. However it feels to be queer in society at large, in the bravado haze of hockey dressing rooms, it will continue to be agonizing for a long, long time.

/

Hockey is a perennial niche sport—it's less watched, less played, and less well understood than basketball, football, and baseball—but it will always have this over its competitors: It's tougher.

When handing out the 2020 Stanley Cup, NHL commissioner Gary Bettman called it the hardest championship win in all of sports: "The gauntlet that you have to run to hoist this trophy is unbelievable."[22] For starters, between the regular season and the playoffs, teams have to play between 98 and 110 games to win the Stanley Cup; in the NFL, the only other genuine contact league of the big four, teams play about a fifth of that number.

Then there's what happens on the ice. Witness the bone-shaking bodychecks, the slashes, collisions, and trips. Witness the bare-knuckle fighting, when the game stops so two players can duke it out, or the brawls, when everyone joins in, even those still on the bench. Hell, witness suit-and-tie-wearing coaches getting into altercations themselves.

Note the way suffering is valorized, the athletes who power through not just pain but debilitating injury: Bobby Baun's broken-ankle overtime game-winner in 1964, Paul Kariya's "Off the floor, on the board!" goal after returning from a devastating check to the head in 2003, Patrice Bergeron playing through a punctured lung in 2013—and those are just moments from the Stanley Cup

22 Nicholas J. Cotsonika, "Bettman Proud of NHL's Accomplishments with Stanley Cup, Hub Cities," NHL, September 29, 2020, https://www.nhl.com/news/commissioner-gary-bettman-proud-of-nhl-accomplishments-with-stanley-cu-319227908.

finals. A YouTube comment on a video compilation of NHL players pushing through pain summed it up thusly: "Soccer players pretend they're hurt, Hockey players pretend they aren't." The comment has over one thousand likes.

So central to the sport is the endurance of pain that the most popular hockey podcast is called *Spittin' Chiclets*—a jokey euphemism for players losing teeth during a game. The average hockey fan may think it's odd to even bring this up, so ingrained is the mentality: Hockey players play through pain because they're real men, and real men aren't pussies. Any deviation from the straight white masculine norm may see a player marked as one. At times, this policing veers into the absurd. In 2018, after his trade from the Calgary Flames, it was suggested that defenceman Dougie Hamilton wasn't a team player because, according to rumours, he was the type of guy who visited museums on his days off.

In 2019, the Carolina Hurricanes caught heat from racist-grandpa-cum-TV-host Don Cherry when the team gathered on home ice to celebrate wins with coordinated dances. "This is the National Hockey League," Cherry said of the Hurricanes' celebratory "storm surges." "They're a bunch of jerks, as far as I'm concerned."[23] These criticisms didn't necessarily represent mainstream hockey opinion, but they did occur in a culture that's oppressively stifling when it comes to difference and flash, one where the banality of players' interview responses (*We've got to work hard, give it 110 percent, get pucks deep*) is legendary.

The era of people like Cherry dogging European players for not measuring up to North American standards of toughness may be over, but within the past two or three years, it's still been reasonable to publicly accuse—in coded hockey terms—straight men of not being straight enough. Players who don't conform are saddled with nicknames like Sidney Crysby or the Sedin Sisters.

The game, of course, is not without its feminine elements. Hockey slang—as much as it celebrates the grind-it-out aspect of the game—can make use of a much more femme lexicon when describing certain plays: A player who stickhandles well has "silky mitts," a good playmaker dishes passes with "soft hands," and some dekes are so technically proficient they become "beautiful." We watch hockey to see the bruisers brawl—but also to see the phenoms dazzle.

Players, commentators, and fans often deal with that contradiction—between the aesthetic beauty of the sport and the innate toughness associated with it—by adding extra masculinity, like a sauce doled out too liberally to cover up an off taste in the dish below.

23 Josh Gold-Smith, "Cherry Rips Hurricanes for Post-Win Celebrations: 'They're a Bunch of Jerks,'" The Score, February 17, 2019, https://www.thescore.com/nhl/news/1718492.

/

Me, I was always a pussy. I came out as bisexual in my late teens and as non-binary in my early thirties, but people could tell that my last name was a misnomer long before I hit puberty. At school and at the rink, they didn't hesitate to let me know.

Growing up in Westmount, Montreal's richest neighbourhood, I played house league. It was nominally coed, but in the decade or so I spent ferrying my equipment to the rink and back, I recall seeing only two girls on the ice. What I remember more than anything, except the smell of the arena and the way raucous voices echoed in the cold air, was the unpleasantness of the boys around me in the dressing room. It worsened as we grew older, peaking during the one season I played in a more competitive league.

I was twelve that year. I didn't know, then, that I wasn't straight or that I wasn't cis—I just knew, as my teammates told me, that I wasn't manly. I was a goaltender, the game's de facto position for weirdos and loners, where every mistake is tallied in the ledger of the scoreboard. I was a class outsider too. Though my parents could afford to live in Westmount's less wealthy lower half, I was nowhere near as well off as many of the other players, the sons of lawyers, business executives, and doctors. My parents didn't own a car, which meant walking to a teammate's house before every road game to carpool. For a while, I borrowed pads and gloves from the home arena. After that, most of my equipment was second-hand and none of it was high-end.

My experience reflects an unpleasant truth about the sport: It costs a lot of money to play. That financial barrier produces a community—both hockey's fans and its elite player pool—that's much more uniformly white than those of the other major North American sports. As Rachel Giese writes in *Boys*, registration in a competitive league can cost hundreds if not thousands of dollars per year, and new equipment can cost hundreds if not thousands more, which requires ample disposable income. (That's not factoring in travel costs for those playing in competitive intercity leagues. Montreal Canadiens goaltender Carey Price's father famously bought a small airplane to ferry his son to and from games when he was growing up in remote Anahim Lake, BC.)

It's hard to build a sport that's accepting of otherness when you start from a base position of excluding the poor—and, in Canada and the US, racialized communities tend to have higher rates of poverty. Basketball, baseball, and soccer don't have especially high barriers for entry—a ball and a hoop, a ball and a bat, or just a ball are all kids need. For hockey, every single player needs a stick and a pair of skates, not to mention a puck and an ice surface.

It's not surprising, then, that hockey is blindingly white and relatively conservative, or that it often stumbles in its attempts to address that fact. In 2020, several Black pro players created the Hockey Diversity Alliance, an NHL-affiliated organization that ended up parting ways with the league months later due to the NHL's perceived failure to address their requests—which included funding for POC-focused grassroots programs and increased use of Black players in promotional materials, among other changes to make the game less exclusionary.

Statistically, hockey is a less predictable sport than its peers are. On any given night, grunt work can have a greater impact than superstar plays, elevating team-first self-sacrifice into dogma. In a culture that valorizes the group over the individual, any kind of difference can and will be weaponized. The toxicity can overflow in ways that are at times criminal, even monstrous.

Consider the pending lawsuit former NHLer Dan Carcillo brought against the Canadian Hockey League, where he played as a teen, about the sexual assaults (in the form of hazing) that he and other rookies had to endure. If rookie players—even those who are cis, straight, white, and normatively masculine—are considered viable targets for in-group/out-group cruelty, what hope do queer kids have of escaping the truncheon?

/

After one year of wearing the white-and-red Westmount Wings jersey, I failed to make the team again. A few years of house league later, in my late teens, I decided to call it quits altogether. Hockey was still fun, still beautiful, still a contest of wits and wills and white-knuckle thrills. But that was on the ice. So long as hockey meant fraternizing with the kinds of boys who played hockey, smelling the acrid scent of their normative masculinity in the dressing room on either end of the game—well, I didn't want to play it that badly.

The aggressive toxicity of hockey culture drove me away from the game I love. I'm not exaggerating when I say I miss it every day, that I daydream about buying all-new goalie equipment someday in the future (when my wallet can take the blow), suiting up, and slowly working my way up to more competitive leagues.

Into my early thirties, I was still imagining what it would be like to be so good, so impenetrable, that they had to sign me to a pro contract despite the fact that, by then, I was already older than half the league. I imagined TV announcers trying to wrap their minds around my use of they/them pronouns. *Well, whatever you wanna call this kid—this guy—he, they—buddy—it—can sure stop the damn puck.*

But, more than the raw facts of sexuality—the feelings of attraction to men, of being outside of full masculinity—there's nothing mainstream hockey culture is so allergic to as queerness. Queerness as ethos, as an intentional going against the grain, not just feeling and wanting differently but *living* differently—this, hockey culture could never abide. If it cannot let a quiet Dougie Hamilton visit museums on his days off without snide commentary, how could it possibly handle queerness?

If ever there are out gay NHL players, I have to imagine they'll be Pete Buttigieg types—practiced not just in crossovers, head-fakes, and taking the body but also in the art of appealing to the mainstream. They'll be in committed relationships, clean-cut, and classically manly. Their teammates will say all the right things: *It's about the logo on your chest, not what happens in your bedroom. He's a stand-up guy and that's all I care about. Gay, straight, bisexual—if he finishes his checks and blocks shots like the rest of us, then what do I care?*

/

In the year since the 2024 American election, many organizations—the NHL among them—have walked back, in ways big and small, prior commitments to different forms of inclusion, diversity, equity, and accessibility. Given hockey's insistence on toughness, it's not hard to imagine the problems I explored in this essay worsening. One thing does give me hope—the birth and growth of the Professional Women's Hockey League. Rising from the ashes of an early 2020s period when there was not a single professional league for women in North America, the PWHL has established itself as a viable league, on the verge of its third season as of this book's publication.

As a Montrealer, I've been lucky enough to attend a couple of Victoire games, and the atmosphere in the crowd is absolutely incredible—a blend of familial love as parents bring children, and a raucous queerness as female pro sports' undeniable lesbian ties become visible. For Christmas last year, my partner (a complete pro sports non-believer) bought us front row tickets to a game against the Toronto Sceptres. Seated directly behind the opposition bench, we had an incredible view of the goings-on, and early on my eyes caught on a single beautiful dangling earring being worn by the backup goalie—just below a dyed blond buzz cut. I looked it up online after the game: It turns out that C.J. Jackson uses they pronouns as well as she. There it was. Someone so like me, getting paid to be a goalie. I almost wept.

/

My favourite bit of NHL propaganda is a thirty-second promotional spot for the 2010 Stanley Cup finals. It's ironic, given my disdain for the ways that hockey players are so often afraid to speak their minds.

Called "No Words," it's an interview montage of players from years past, fresh off winning the Cup, trying and failing to put the sensation into sentences. As a soft melody plays over the clips, we watch the men pause and stammer and swallow. One pinches the bridge of his nose; another stares upward, trying to will away tears.

It's a beautiful, less-is-more revelation that achieving glory in this kid's game is genuinely, unquantifiably meaningful for these men. In this moment of triumph, they're reduced to shy little boys—a silence born not of caginess but of awe, the lessons about being a tough guy stripped away and replaced with a humanity that feels raw and tender. I cannot watch it without getting goosebumps.

The truth is, there has always been homoerotic desire in hockey, the way there is any time enough men gather together, like a sort of queer holy spirit. *Whenever two or more gather in my name, I am there.* It may not have been spoken aloud, acted on, or acknowledged, but it was there, the way queerness has always been, uninvited yet irrepressible.

As Pierre LeBrun wrote in *The Athletic* in 2020, in an article about the coming out of player agent Bayne Pettinger, Pettinger's brother Matt thinks he "undoubtedly had a gay teammate at some point" during his NHL playing career.[24] It's hard not to believe him—almost 2,300 men played at least one game in the league over that ten-year period.

I imagine a player in the sixties or seventies—bushy moustache, sideburns, perhaps a goalie, like me—sitting in the dressing room for an older franchise. The Red Wings, maybe, or the Flyers—a meat-and-potatoes team. Silently carrying a truth he knows about himself as his teammates talk about their sex lives: wives, girlfriends, mistresses, so-called puck bunnies. Putting on his

24 Pierre LeBrun, "A Young NHL Player Agent Comes Out, Supported by Hockey's Biggest Stars," November 5, 2020, *The Athletic*, https://www.nytimes.com/athletic/2178746/2020/11/05/nhl-player-agent-comes-out/.

jockstrap, his chest protector, his mask. Ready to go out and prove how tough he is all over again. How unafraid. How much a real man, in every sense of the word.

It is choosing they/them pronouns in 2014, the moment Facebook gave users the option, telling myself it was a move of allyship. How did I buy that one? It is trying on my first pair of American Apparel skinny jeans in 2006 or so, Slim Slack in navy blue size 32, so tight, hugging, how right that felt. It is how adversarial my relationships with anger and arousal have always been. How scared I am of being angry or horny—those Man feelings. How wrong they felt on me. How quickly I tried to transmute anger into sadness. The work I put in to hide my desire from others. It is being gendered as anything femme of centre wavering between feeling like a beautiful compliment and one I don't deserve.

EGO SVM LVX MVNDI

I believed in God as a kid bc I always felt so moved during worship songs at my megachurch and then I went to a One Direction concert and felt the same thing and realized I just like live music
—@likethabug, TikTok

I always thought it was "Our father who aren't *in heaven."*
—my dad

"IN THE BEGINNING" was how I wanted to start it.

It seemed important to me that the first three words of my follow-up poetry collection be the first three words commonly used in the opening phrase of the English-language translations of the Bible.

The collection was meant to be an exploration of the ways religious faith and romantic love had overlapped in my life, the way parachuting into the yawning maw of a newly godless universe around the age of eighteen had left a spiritual void in my life that I turned to the roller-coaster intensity of young love to fill. It was, in some ways, about a specific relationship I'd had over the course of fourteen months between the ages of twenty and twenty-two; in others, it was about the scars that a breakup can leave on your psyche when you invest the relationship that led to it with the weight of the world entire.

I wanted to call it "EGO SVM LVX MVNDI," *I am the light of the world,* an inscription I'd encountered in an art history class years earlier that felt so beautiful it felt right, even though I couldn't explain its seeming self-centredness in a way that ever felt perfectly satisfying. Its wrongness, its obvious literal egocentrism a kind of rhyme for the username I'd been taking with me to each new successive social network I joined over the years: alex_icon, alex icon, a lexicon. Smiling as people ribbed me about it. A collection of words, an image, me.

The slipperiness of the idea, the concept behind it, was how easily it felt like romantic love could replace religious faith, how much a fetish for pattern and coincidence pivoted from meaning God was real to meaning she and I were right for each other. *I am the light of the world*, says Jesus to his followers. *You are the apple of my eye*, I say to my love.

The theme of the book was religion because religion was where I came from. I'd attended the same church in Montreal—St. Stephen's Anglican, a venerable nineteenth-century edifice on the corner of René-Lévesque and Atwater—every Sunday from the age of about three months to sometime in my eighteenth year. In addition to the Sunday morning pilgrimages, I started going to the church youth group Friday evenings around the age of twelve or thirteen, and continued attending every week until I was around seventeen. On top of that, I went to a week-long sleepaway Christian camp in Quebec's Eastern Townships two or three times as a teen.

As a child, my faith led, before long, to philosophical inquiry. I remember grappling with the idea that it was impossible not to sin, probably around the age of ten or eleven. What if I was really, really dedicated, though? Are there certain types of people, certain forms of neurodivergence, that are predisposed to religiosity? Maybe some people shouldn't be exposed to dogma; maybe people with predilections for addictive behaviour shouldn't be exposed to certain drugs. How does faith intersect with madness? I never really paid much attention to the idea that sinning was a necessary part of the equation. I would just try harder. I would just try harder.

In my thirties, I read a young non-binary lesbian's essay about the ways their OCD mapped onto their Catholic upbringing. The way religion is so full of rites, things to repeat over and over. I think about the couple's son in Nabokov's short story "Symbols and Signs," perhaps my favourite assigned reading from undergrad. Held in a mental institution, unable to stop seeing patterns in things, the way everything is connected for him. "Referential mania." Was it so different from the way I saw the world at the time? A difference of degree, not of kind.

In any case, everywhere I looked, there was God. The world was a palace of wonders. *In my Father's house are many rooms*, and they all held treasures to be discovered. The faces of the beautiful girls I had crushes on—Carmen, Gabrielle, Fanny, Charlotte. The taste of fruit punch. The way LEGO blocks fit together. The way the Canadiens players skated, ballet on ice. Snow, the way there was so much of it here in Montreal, the banks of white taller than I was, deep into the winter. Learning to bike in the summer, my father tempting me through the fear with promises of an ice cream bar. Being brave enough to hold a candle with everyone else while we sang "This Little Light of Mine" a cappella under the dark night sky at Christian summer camp. The hand flex in *Pride & Prejudice* (2005).

/

Around the age of eleven or twelve, I stopped having birthday parties.

Between then and the year I turned thirty-one, I didn't throw myself a single party. Twice, friends threw me surprise ones: the friend group I took the bus with showed up at my house in the morning before school when I turned seventeen, and in my mid-twenties, a birthday dinner with just one friend turned out to be a group affair. But those were exceptions, blips in an otherwise solid narrative—that I was weird, and fragile, and different from other people, and that I could not enjoy the things that they enjoyed.

Going on anti-anxiety medication four or five months before I turned thirty changed that. With the exception of two birthdays—due to a COVID scare and a bedbug infestation—I've thrown a party for myself every year since. In my mid-thirties, I'm now at an age where it no longer feels necessary or expected, but there's a part of me that feels like I'm making up for lost time.

Growing up, though, they made me feel so bad. Birthdays, because of the specialness, set my child mind aroar with expectation. The presents I would receive, the friendship, nay, the adulation, my peers would bestow on me—but real life never lived up to young Alex's fantasies. Before long, I learned that it was easier not to get excited in the first place. If there was no celebration happening, then I knew exactly what I was getting.

This was a sort of microcosm for my relationship with my peers when I was growing up. I was always estranged, alienated, strange, alien. Off to the side. My relationship with the kids I went to church with was better than my relationship with those I went to school with, but not radically different. Here, I was an interloper in a smaller group; I felt less marginalized, but the remaining distance then was all the more painful, pound for pound. Because it was a much smaller group; because we had chosen to be here, sort of, to some degree; and because Christians were supposed to be kind. What was wrong with me? I wondered.

Of course I was friendly with some of them; David's father gave me rides to hockey games and Matty always greeted me with a smile. I didn't see myself in Mark and Brodie but we got along all right enough, the way boys do. The people whose attention I craved the most were a trio of girls whose names all began with C. They seemed to have bonded in a way that precluded the entry of others into their circle, though in retrospect that might just have been a sheen of projection, a story I told myself to dull the pain of feeling excluded. I did have a regular-style crush on one of them, whose blond wispiness tinged with an aura of sadness I would recognize in many subsequent crushes over the years. But it wasn't just that, I knew even then. What part of me, exactly, cared that they didn't seem to want to talk to me? Did I want to have a girls' night sleepover with them? Did I want to be in their confidence, engage in hours-long MSN Messenger conversations, know and be known? I wanted to be accepted. To be seen as not-other. By them and not by the boys. For reasons I didn't understand yet. Wouldn't for decades.

/

I'm not sure when exactly I realized I was neurodivergent. For starters, that term wasn't in widespread use until my late twenties, long after my first interactions with the reality that my brain worked differently—worse, it often seemed to me—than other people's. In late 2007, when government PSA billboards in the Metro reached out and gently suggested that it might be depression. In early 2008, not long after writing my first and thus far only suicide note, when I sought help from my university's health centre, filling out forms, answering in-person questions, being set up with a therapist. A year or two later, when a friend sent me an online "autism test" and I scored a single point below the range in which the test-taker was thought to probably have autism. In 2012 or thereabouts, when a friend of my mother's posited that I might have ADHD, though I brushed this off, not knowing much about the diagnosis beyond the hyperactive young boy stereotype. Other quirks of my brain. Stuff like how it felt like other people never knew who I was or remembered me. A kind of missing object permanence of the self. In the mid-2010s, at my job, when successive managers wondered aloud during performance reviews, year after year, why I never seemed to reach my potential, why I was always behind schedule, my work always rushed. In 2018 when I got my first prescription for fluoxetine, an anti-anxiety medication better known as Prozac, reminding me of nothing so much as the scene in Heather O'Neill's

Lullabies for Little Criminals when Baby finally tries heroin—a human being finally touching down on the alien planet of a substance they were destined since birth to come home to. The wailing and gnashing of teeth. How I'd been primed to see it as *bad*. Because of all the leftist Gen X anti-pharmaceutical propaganda I'd absorbed as a teenage reader of *Adbusters*. And how a few weeks later, while walking down des Pins toward Avenue du Parc, I noticed it had changed things, and now I was a little bit less afraid of everything. *Oh*, I thought. *It worked*. I kept walking east.

Of course, if either I or my parents had had a more robust understanding of mental health, it wouldn't have taken until 2018, or 2008, or maybe even 1998 for some form of psychiatric or medical intervention to occur. But they were not bad about it; they were just people who'd grown up in a time that did not yet understand these things. And, if we're being honest, themselves each strange enough that my own strangeness did not seem out of place. It's the way things are passed down. The *mise en abyme* realization when going through a family photo album—that we are just slightly altered versions of our parents, and they, slightly altered versions of their parents, and on, and on, and on. I wonder how it might have gone in another time and place. So many cultures would have been harsher on me, but it's heartening sometimes to remember that there were ones that saw neurodivergent people as prophets, messengers of the gods, something holy.

/

For the fourteen months we dated between August 2009 and October 2010, it was beautiful and brimming with meaning. I was self-consciously romantic, trying to impress her at every turn, investing the relationship with a weight it did not deserve to have to hold. I was a being of pure romantic gesture, for a time. I was poems, unannounced visits, pebbles thrown against her window, a message written on a T-shirt with fabric paint, a papier-mâché heart made out of red Metro tickets. I bought the male counterpart to her childhood doll, kidnapped her original, and enlisted a mutual friend to take pictures of the two canoodling in places we'd kissed around the city. I couldn't help it. The coincidences all felt meaningful. That was part of the problem, part of why I cared so much about that relationship, beyond the things her face did to me, the way it felt when we kissed, the way our conversations were filled with jokes and wordplay and longing and an appreciation for beauty. The fact that we'd gone to the same elementary school, though we'd never met then, of course, not with me being four years older. The fact that we'd met because we were each friends with a different sibling from the same family. The fact that after I moved out of my parents' place at eighteen, the home I'd lived in for the past decade, her family moved in just three or four doors down. How we'd been nearly neighbours. If that wasn't a sign of something, what was? Of course, I didn't know at the time how inconsequential these kinds of coincidences were, how they really pointed above all else to the fact that our parents had chosen the same affluent neighbourhood to raise children in, that being neighbours was one of the primary ways people met romantic partners in the twentieth century, that I was just engaging in some form of apophenia all over again, replacing one system of universal symbolism and meaning with another. I still believed.

/

One of the most important things in my life at a young age was being, feeling, seeming smart. It was at odds with doctrine and, more importantly, the general vibe of faith. This was one of the things that made my break from the church easier, maybe. How little people at church seemed to care about writing. Typos and spelling mistakes and grammar errors in seemingly every bit of text I saw shown on the church projector. My child mind could not comprehend why they hadn't put more effort into getting it right. Wasn't this stuff important? I'm not sure I ever framed it this way explicitly, but it sort of felt like an insult to God. Language was so central to my experience of religion. The strange formulations that got stuck in the teeth of my mind's craw, products of the fact that the text we used was an ancient translation of an ancient document written in a radically different language. The syntax garbled, the word choices odd, unexpected. At times the meanings themselves hard to parse: *In the beginning was the Word, and the Word was with God, and the Word was God.* And how text, how writing, now held the stories—the whale, the flood, the pillar of salt, what the fire did to the cities, what the slingshot did to the giant, what the beautiful woman did to the king. Was it a sin to care too much about words? No one can serve two masters. Though one time someone did suggest that maybe there was a future for me as a pastor. And I did, in time, grow to feel comfortable speaking in front of crowds. *For wherever two or three are gathered in my name, I am there among them.*

I remember the leader of my youth group telling me she'd had a dream about me, a dream about my faith. Christian camp leaders answering questions about whether masturbation was a sin or not. Telling us it wasn't, if you could do it without thinking sinful thoughts. But you couldn't. Realistically. A church parent who didn't usually run Sunday school pressed into service telling us *Harry Potter* books were bad news (they are, as it would turn out, not because they're about witchcraft but for reasons that wouldn't have been explicable to my younger self in the very early days of the twenty-first century). A counsellor at the day camp I was attending in a sort of "assistant counsellor" capacity admonishing me in front of everyone for repeatedly wanting to play his djembe during worship song portions. Confessing to my mother that I masturbated a lot, and her asking my godfather what he thought about the issue from a religious standpoint, since my own father was an atheist now. My godfather's response coming back to me through my mother, a kind of fumbled hedging, soft around the edges, telegraphing that I wasn't *exactly* a bad person. That maybe this stuff was complicated after all. Another kid at church confessing to me how impossible it felt. To not masturbate. And me telling him. "Well. My godfather said it was maybe not the end of the world."

/

At some point in my thirties, I asked my mom about what brought her to the church. I knew my dad's parents had brought him to church, that there had been at least a handful of times from his youth when his memories were lit up with stained glass. But my mother was clearly the driving force behind our churchgoing—where had that come from? It was unclear whether there'd been any religion in her childhood, if it was something she felt herself coming back to, relapsing into, returning to the fold of. But no. Her parents, self-styled intellectuals, rejected that kind of stuff. The truth almost made me laugh. How unexpected it was for me—pedestrian, prosaic. Out of the blue, out of left field. She had just been lonely as a young adult. Was invited to church by people at university. Had found a community, acceptance within a group, a new feeling for her after a lifetime of feeling like an outsider, for reasons she wouldn't put a name to for many more decades. Here, in Ottawa, in the early 1980s, at church, she felt a sense of being welcomed, of being welcome. And began to believe, over time, in the holiness of that feeling. This is one of the crucial bait and switches of religion. She kept with it for a few more decades because the good feeling never entirely left, 'til I was old enough to believe on my own. Funny to think about in the context of the role religion played in my life. All the spiritual guilt I ever felt, all the grappling and wrestling with faith

I'd gone through—Jacob and the angel—was because my mom had had trouble making friends as a kid. This is why—and how—people find themselves in cults. Just lucky my mom's cult happened to be the Anglican church. Fairly porous, as cults go. And there were maple cookies after the service was over. And in time I came to understand how hard it would have been for her to say no to that feeling. How our needs, our judgment shifts when we go too long without things. Maslow's hierarchy of the self.

/

I noticed the little tics of TikTok, the faint traces of traits you'd never guess meant anything until you run across them out in the world, contextualized, and know. Like watching a trailer for a documentary on autistic kids in 2006 or 2007 and seeing a child do something, a little repetitive hand movement, a digital blur, and going, *Oh, I do that too*. Only when no one's looking, only when I'm deep in thought. But yes, I do that. Still, to this day. A hand at each side of the face, a quick vibration. They call it stimming, it turns out. Or how autistic people love to quote things, love to speak in movie and TV and song lyric references. The same lines coming back again over and over, finding new life in fresh contexts.

In any case, everywhere I looked, there was beauty. I wrote in a poem once that trees, blue whales, and Jesus lizards, if you looked at them in a certain light, were alien. Complex, magnificent life forms living on a unique planet floating through space. In calling them "alien" I was attempting to recast the familiar as strange. But maybe what I meant was "holy." The hummingbird, the flying jewel. The black opal in *Uncut Gems*. "Casimir Pulaski Day" by Sufjan Stevens. The human-made wonders of the world. Pyramids. Hagia Sophia. Musée d'Orsay. The pre-colonial names of the natural ones: Uluru. Chomolungma. Mosi-oa-Tunya, *the smoke that thunders*. The way in Montreal, Prince-Arthur intersected with Durocher. *He had to pull the sword from the stone to become king*. "JOAN BAEZ ~ The Lily Of The West ~" on YouTube sent to me by someone named Flora. When first falling in love.

There were moments of grace moving (walking or biking) along De Maisonneuve, near Roslyn, and feeling the interconnectedness of all things, the beautiful design of it, God's plan, safe in the middle of an upper-class suburb. My anxiety needing there to be an order to the universe. A feeling coming over me in the car, middle back seat, sensing the precarity of feeling closer to the windshield, after a camp counsellor had put on OK *Computer* and I heard—without realizing I'd heard—opening lyrics about a car crash, a minute into a car ride. Thinking, *It would be okay if I died right now.* The peace of the Lord, which transcends all understanding. Somehow safe because I was surrounded by faith. Though I'm glad I didn't. So many truths I hadn't yet learned, so many things I hadn't yet experienced. What it felt like to be published. What it felt like to bike up the mountain. What it felt like to be shortlisted for awards. To win one. For my writing. What it felt like to have a Christmas dinner with both my divorced parents at once. What it felt like to get a real job as an editor. What it felt like to give a speech at a dear friend's wedding. What it felt like to make someone squirt. A certain irrefutable truth to it. She'd been sitting on my face. So: like getting rained on. *Oh,* I thought. *It worked. E pur si muove.*

/

In the fall of 2012, for a creative writing class on memoir, I am required to submit a piece for workshop. I am twenty-four years old. With the deadline approaching and no good ideas springing forth, I begin, late one night, to type away at a new piece of writing. A story from my life. I find myself recounting the arc of my last relationship. The one with a teenager, that seemed impossibly significant and terribly romantic. It is late, the day before it is due, then after midnight, the day it is due. This is the way it is with writing, sometimes—we don't write what we want to write, but what comes out. There is a voice that says, *Just write this now, you can deal with the consequences later*. I am listening to the voice, the words are flying out of me, and they are taking shape in an interesting form. I find the piece has a kind of tone that is new for me, and—also new for me—that it is good. When I am done the piece is around six thousand words long, one of the longest pieces, maybe the single longest, that I have ever produced in my eleven semesters of creative writing thus far. It is a piece that juxtaposes the emotional intensity of my experience with a certain spareness of narrative language, that elegantly makes use of reference, that dances in a certain way. It uses the first-person singular in the present tense, which makes everything feel immediate in a way that I like. Though the story is about a relationship with a seventeen-year-old and makes mention of our sex, I email it to my professor, and he shares it with my classmates. That week, as I sit down in class, preparing for the discussion on my piece, a cute classmate gushes over one detail in it, a religious reference she connects with, about my first visit to the girl's home.

> She asks if she can touch my Adam's apple, which is just big enough to be noticeably bigger than average. I nod, and swallow while her finger is on it, up and down. She gives a little squeal. It is the first time, I think, that we touch. Original sin.

The class discussion that follows is a mixed one, but despite my habit of focusing on the negatives when I'm being workshopped, here, all I seem to hear is praise. I know in my head this is good writing. Better yet, as far as I can tell, it's not cribbing from anything obvious, anything that belongs too strongly to anyone else. I am that I am. I've stumbled into something and now I never have to give it back.

/

The final decision, I remember, took place at night, in bed, in the bedroom of the home I spent my eighth to eighteenth years in. It felt, in retrospect, a bit like another decision I made over and over in that room—the decision to, finally, yes, give in to desire, and begin to touch myself, knowing where that would lead, though I did and didn't want to pass through that dark tunnel into the light of orgasm. A world I remember coming into my head unbidden, not long after I started experiencing these things that everyone loves to point out the French sometimes call *le petit mort*, the little death, around the age of ten, in the same home, at the back of the house, top or bottom bunk, I can't remember, before we switched the bedrooms around to accommodate for my sister and I growing up and needing separate spaces. But this night, seventeen or eighteen, travelling inexorably down (or up) a tunnel, also in my mind, though not really in my body, toward a realization, a *mise en abyme*, the sky opening up below me, infinite, no safety net. A void. Darkness was over the surface of the deep.

I don't believe there is a God.

Truly I tell you, this very night, before the rooster crows, you will deny me three times.

There is no God.

There isn't.

And then there wasn't. And everything was still there. Same as before. The Earth, not formless and void, but rotating on its axis, a little under 1,700 kilometres per hour, slowly making its way around the sun.

I ran with this feeling and didn't look back. I never went to church again. I started trying to convince my mother, which didn't take much work. I smouldered. In my new life as an atheist I was full of anger. Anger at having been lied to by so many, anger at having bought it so deeply, for so long. I ported the faith I'd had in God to a new faith in His absence. I was still dogmatic, too sure of myself, and full of contempt for non-non-believers.

At some point, walking home from a party, perhaps, likely in my early twenties, I remember saying aloud to the empty, tree-lined street the forbidden words: "I renounce the Holy Spirit." I had read somewhere that that was an unretractable weapon of a phrase, the one thing you could do that would prevent you from entering into heaven, no matter what else you did or avoided doing in life, no matter how many times you apologized. I said it as a matter of faith: I did not believe in heaven. I did believe in its absence, enough to engage in a sort of rite about it.

/

Why did I want everything to be so important as a teenager? I was so scared of being meaningless, just another snowflake in the storm, a dot in a pointillist painting. Everything at that age seemed tinged with a desire to be written about in history books, to be remembered, not just known now but known through time, a little teenage Ozymandias. I told friends I wanted to be the world's first pregnant man (foreshadowing). I told friends I wanted to die at fifty-five by assassination. I thrilled to books about the political and social upheavals of the twentieth century. My first Gmail account was us.versus.them@gmail.com. I listened to Rage Against the Machine a lot.

All this while still a Christian. I wanted so badly for things to be important. God was one way for that to be true. The Bible so full of epic moments. Blinded Samson pulling down the temple pillars in his rage. The trumpets shaking the walls of Jericho to ruins. I accuse Judas, in the Garden, with the Kiss. *Eloi, eloi, lama sabachthani?* A sequence of words I can spell without checking, know by heart, the Roman rendering of the original Aramaic.

In truth, as a neurodivergent person brought up in the church, I got lucky in some ways. The ways in which my brain works strangely did, I think, lead to a surfeit of devotion, but my parents had led me to a comparatively low-stakes version of Christianity, and let me free inside its gated fields rather than riding me like an ox. My brain strangenesses didn't dovetail with the many potentially harmful facets of faith as neatly as they could have. And after I'd given it all up, some of the issues persisted. Was that a sign of religious faith's ill effects remaining tattooed into the fabric of me, or was it a sign that the behavioural tics were never really its fault to begin with?

As feminism became my new devotion in my twenties, for instance, my masturbatory guilt shifted from feeling like I'd let God down to feeling like I'd visited something horrible upon the subjects of my fantasies. Every time I touched myself while thinking about a classmate, a co-worker, a writer I was in community with, my pleasure was tinged with a vulgar feeling. Not because of the act of masturbation, the inherent lewdness of it, but because I was a Man and they were Women. I was the thing that was Bad, and my engaging in self-pleasure was at their expense. This was not a fun or healthy relationship with the practice. I worried that I was somehow poisoning my relationship with these women in my life, worried that the contents of my fantasies would somehow, imperceptibly, leak through into the way I treated them, noxious gases, worried about the weight of these private behaviours on, for lack of a better word, my soul. In short, I worried that I was sinning.

Was that religious guilt carrying on its long tradition even in its own absence, an abusive father whose family members still enact his toxicities after he's been buried? *Yea, though I walk through the valley of the shadow.*

/

I kept on thinking, feeling, and writing about that one relationship for three quarters of a decade, five times the length of time it had ever existed in the first place, an absurd ratio. But of course it meant too much when it had been asked to fill a hole the size of a god. Of course it wasn't healthy. The one thing I'm proud of is that I did not spend those seven years haranguing my ex with the weight of my regret and my longing. She was younger than me—too young by some accounts—and did not need or deserve my ugly sadness in her life. Finally, in early 2018, I asked if we could have coffee and talk about what happened, because I realized I needed that to move on, and she obliged. A few weeks after the coffee I had my moment of realization: *Oh, the weight is gone.* The conversation had worked, had melted the sadness out of my life, had sublimated the heaviness into steam. *Oh*, I thought. *It worked.* Like magic. I moved on.

/

When I was thirty-five I decided to face the question head-on. Diagnoses are never cures, but having the words for who and how and what you are can be such a balm. The guilt I had felt growing up, my perception of myself as having led such a privileged life completely free of pain or trauma, because I'd never been physically or sexually abused, my parents had stayed together almost to my twenties, and I'd never gone hungry, my relatives all still alive. Finally, in my thirties, getting to acknowledge that being non-binary and neurodivergent, always feeling othered, wrong, and ashamed, was a meaningful hurt on its own. In addition to having anxiety and ADHD and possibly depression, I told my doctor that I thought I might be autistic. I told him that I knew these conditions were often comorbid, that as I'd learned more about autism in recent years online I'd started to see more and more things line up, people describing symptoms I hadn't known were symptoms, commonalities of experience, things like my urge to tidy up the piles in bookstores, how I eat in particular ways that don't always make sense to others, that I'd had a stim since childhood. I wasn't sure of anything, of course, but there were enough suggestive pieces of evidence that it felt worth looking into, maybe, and I asked him what I should do if I wanted to know for sure whether I did or did not have autism. He told me that it could cost up to $2,000 to be tested, so unless I felt like I needed to know that badly, and if I was already functioning well enough to lead the life I wanted, it might not be worth the trouble. The book of poems, for its part, remains unpublished.

It is the fact that when I listen to music, the singer is more often a man, but when I put a song on repeat, when I listen to the same thing over and over and over again, trying to capture a lightning spark of feeling in a jar—those songs are almost only ever by women. All of Sade's hits, "Bad Romance"–era Lady Gaga, post–"Call Me Maybe" Carly Rae (though of course "Call Me Maybe" is a bop too), early-period Taylor, a handful of Cher singles, "Teenage Dream," "New Rules," "Hello," "How Will I Know," "Physical," "It's All Coming Back to Me Now," "Side to Side" feat. Nicki Minaj, "It Ain't Me" feat. Kygo, "Lights" by Ellie Goulding. Not just for the bubbling poppiness but for the small spark of transgressive glee I feel at how much I like these girly, girly, girly songs.

Hallowed Out

LIKE BIRTHDAYS, I stopped celebrating Halloween around the age of eleven or twelve.

By the time I was thirteen, I had sworn it off entirely. I was still in my devout Christian era, but my objections to the celebration of witches and horror had nothing to do with religious doctrine or dogma.

It was about fear.

That's the point of Halloween, isn't it? It's spooky season, after all. But where other kids seemed to delight in this, like passengers on a roller coaster feeling exhilarated by the terror, for me, it was distinctly unpleasant, and the weirdness of feeling out of step with everyone else was a second, ancillary unpleasantness, one that blossomed in particular in my twenties as going out on Halloween became a de rigueur social event.

During that period, failing to come up with an elaborate costume became proof that one was irredeemably boring—the more so in queer circles, where "gay Halloween" and its focus on increasingly niche things to dress up as became so culturally entrenched that it turned into a meme. I hate gay Halloween. What do you mean you're going as the '80s synthpop–inspired mourning fugue-state fever dream of a college professor from a late 2000s animated web short?

As a kid, I wasn't afraid of witches, ghosts, or skeletons. Black cats, spiders, and bats did not set my spine tingling. What scared me about Halloween, then and now, was something that at the time I felt alone in, though I have come to learn others experience it too: the fear of people in costume.

I could sense then that costumes had a kind of power. That people donned them and became different somehow. Of course, this is exactly the draw of Halloween: becoming who you're not, tapping into something else, the thrill of stepping into a new body, a new social position, a new self.

For younger me, this was terrifying. Whatever laws and rules ordered the universe that I was growing up in, Halloween—whether a day, a week, or a month—was a time period in which they were defunct. For someone still doing their best to figure out how social interaction worked, Halloween was a full-on capital-*P* Purge. Nothing was safe, no one could be trusted, anarchy reigned.

So deeply was this fear embedded in me at the time that I found I could not manage to enjoy Halloween as an adult, and feeling left out of its increasingly celebrated place within modern queerness left me feeling a strange kind of hollow. To feel excluded from a community composed of people who themselves so often felt like outcasts from the wider society—this was a strange, disorienting double-minority feeling. If I couldn't feel included here, could I feel included anywhere?

/

I remember three specific moments of fear from childhood Halloweens that led to my break with the holiday. Two were on my street, a handful of metres from my house each time; one was a few minutes' walk away, along the street that intersected ours to the south.

The first two, in retrospect, feel comparatively anodyne. One was an instance of my costume's cape fluttering over an open flame—a candle left out on a neighbour's porch for lighting and spooky ambience. Nothing happened—there was no fire, no singing smell, no stop, drop, and roll—just an indelible moment of fear, something in me clenching shut.

At that age, I saw fire much the same way I saw people wearing costumes: unknowable, unpredictable, and dangerous. I did not yet grasp that it obeyed physical laws, that passing something quickly over a flame meant that a current of air moved the flame to the side, that you could move your own hand side to side over a candle without even feeling pain.

The second was the year before, or after, from across our street, after dark. A man sat up from under a pile of leaves on a lawn and roared, sending nearby children into shrieks. He must have been a neighbour. A father, perhaps, of children I played street hockey with, a man my father's age. I can recognize now that he was being playful, getting into the spirit of things. Perhaps some of the sidewalk shrieks came from his own kids. Maybe they were delighted by the prank. Maybe he was being a good dad.

At the time, what I saw was a grown man carrying out a plan to scare children and, in my case, succeeding. He was acting unpredictably, his behaviour wildly inappropriate on any other night of the year. It wasn't fun. It stayed with me.

/

What does it mean to want to dress up as someone—or something—else? How much time, money, effort goes into making a costume? Stitching, ironing, trying on, modelling in front of the mirror. Undoing, redoing, not quite liking how it looks. Putting in the work to get it right, or giving up and wearing it out, imperfect? How much thought, how much care? How whole do people feel when they see themselves anew like this? How different is it from the process of creating one's everyday look? The way so many queer people have to disguise themselves as cishet. The way so many queer people get to disguise themselves as whatever they want. At a certain point, the costume is the true self. Bruce Wayne, Clark Kent, that kind of thing. Which was more me wearing a disguise: me putting on femme accessories or makeup, or me wearing boring men's clothes all the time?

And what do the things we choose to disguise ourselves as say about us? Kids dressing up as superheroes and princesses, a jock dressing up as a beautiful woman, or the son of a prime minister dressing up as a person of colour. Halloween an opening in the fabric of reality. Disguises part of the long history of human existence. Ancient masks uncovered by archaeologists. WWII photos on Tumblr of British soldiers in drag. Me, age six or seven, homemade Spider-Man in a balaclava, a red cagoule, eight-legged logo drawn in black marker. The daisy-chain links of human behaviour throughout time.

/

The third and final moment of fear that I remember came on the last Halloween I celebrated, except for two exceptions, blips in an otherwise solid narrative. It was around four in the afternoon, and I, eleven or twelve, was hurrying to the hockey arena a few blocks away to borrow the goalie equipment I would wear to my team's away game that evening from the rink's equipment manager, as my parents were unable to afford a set for me.

I remember that I was wearing an oversized, baby-blue toque that an aunt had knit for me and walking in a noticeably odd way, timing my footfalls to land right before and after the sidewalk cracks, such that my stride became a kind of Morse code—short, long, short, long—a practice that I've slipped into here and there over the course of my life whenever I'm walking.

From across the street, two older boys, well into their teens and significantly bigger and stronger than me, noticed what must have seemed a strange sight: my large sky-blue head, my hands jammed in my pockets, and my lunatic gait, my little legs stretching to make up the length of each sidewalk square and then immediately doing a much shorter hop as I danced my feet around the lines in the cement.

What they recognized was prime material for bullying. They crossed the street and, in an instant, there was one on each side of me, their arms across my shoulders, trapping me in a new three-person unit.

The silly walk disappeared, replaced by pure, unalloyed fear. I didn't know or recognize these guys, and they had singled me out, initiating an interaction over which I had no control and into which I had no insight. I don't remember what they said to kick things off—only what one of them said at the end of the conversation a few metres farther down the road. I believe I asked them, somehow, why they were now flanking me, to which one of them, in a voice whose put-on raspy timbre I still precisely recall, responded, "Because we want to fuck you."

Instinct took over. In a split second, I dropped my shoulders from beneath their arms, spun around, and tore off back in the direction of home, for the first time feeling like I was in one of those terrible children's stories I'd read so many of, where the protagonist has to escape from peril.

I also remember their response: laughter. How humiliating, to be rewarded for your daring escape with the aggressors' boast that it was all in fun and you had never been in any real danger at all. I was eleven or twelve, and this was my first experience with sexual cruelty. At some point between hearing the word *fuck* uttered aloud in a threatening way and the next October 31st, something in me closed the door on Halloween. It was not and had never been a safe time to be outside. It was a time—a day, a season—that drove people to a certain kind of madness.

Of course, whether its being Halloween factored in any way into the two boys' decision to give me a scare remains unknowable. Famously, teenage boys interested in wreaking havoc on those around them do not restrict themselves to cordoned-off times and places within which misbehaviour is sanctioned. They might have done the same thing to me, or to someone else, any other day of the year. I very much doubt that either of those two people would remember this moment, one that's been seared into me for nearly a quarter century. It was a lark, the kind of thing teenage boys might do on unthinking dares all the time. Perhaps this was an aberration for one or both, or perhaps they did similar or much worse things to other people before and/or after that Halloween.

It is not hard for me to imagine, in retrospect, a world where the one older boy's specific choice to go to a sexual place was indicative of something more interesting, more human, than just wanting to be monstrous for a moment. Was he uttering an unsayable desire for intimacy with the other boy, using me—unconsciously, unknowingly—as an intermediate? Was he someone who had been victimized in one way or another like this in the past and taking on the role of predator rather than prey, a twisted stab at healing?

/

Somehow, it feels like the whole of my relationship to Halloween runs through the lens of the things that made me different from the other people I knew when I was growing up—things that were unsayable, or at least unknowable, if not indescribable at the time, but have since resolved into relatively neat definitions: queer (bisexual, non-binary) and neurodivergent (anxiety, ADHD, possible autism spectrum, high functioning).

Before I had the words it was just a morass, an ugly space of a palpable negativity that crept into view as the calendar flipped to October, something I could not narrativize into a pleasing answer for decades. I don't know. I just don't like Halloween. I was not, I think, recalling those three moments of fear, or other negative reactions to being out and about on the 31st. It was just feeling a feeling, something in the pit of me.

The pain of my mismatch with Halloween's pull only increased over the years, as it went from being a matter of mainstream culture to one that freaks like me were supposed to enjoy even more than the normies. I watched everyone

I loved revel in its black-and-orange glory. I felt alone in my discomfort. That schoolyard feeling again. I was a sad, pathetic loser whose habit of spending the night in, heartbeat elevated at the thought of the outside, marked me.

Gay Halloween isn't the only aspect of contemporary queer culture that made me feel incredibly alone, though—Pride parades do too. Though, on the surface, the vibes of the two occasions are quite different—a kind of dialectic: dark/bright, eerie/fun, day/night, colourful/sombre—for queer people they can have much in common: an annual opportunity to dress up, to show out, to come together, to reject the conformity of straight culture's jacket. For me, the sensation of being overwhelmed by crowds at each proved equally good at keeping me away. How was I so bad at being queer? At times, my neurodivergence, which felt like an important part of my non-binariness, has felt like an immovable fact standing in the way of my acceptance into the alphabet mafia, too. Too crazy to be cis, and too crazy to be queer, as well. A secret third thing.

My Pride parade was staying home. My LGBTQ was talking to one other person and letting them be my whole world for an hour or two. As I posted on Bluesky once, "Not gay as in attracted to people of the same gender, queer as in there's something just a little … *off* … about me." I could not fathom losing myself on dance floors, in crowds, raves, clubs, marches, the subject of a thousand imagined glances, trapped in a net with a real psychic weight. Whenever I was in a crowd, whether one I felt congruous with or one I felt scared of, I was always at least a little bit tense.

I felt like a bad gay. How bound up in shame and otherness I was, that Pride itself felt alienating. And yet Halloween, in many ways its vibe apogee, I was equally repelled by, a spinning magnet caught between two forms of queerness I could not manage to hack.

/

It didn't help that I never really found anything I wanted to dress up as. The two times I did go out as an adult, each an instance of my caving to a different significant other's desire to attend a costume party, I fashioned almost comically genderless outfits, turning a white pillowcase into the STM's new red-and-blue Metro ticket in 2009, and then turning another white pillowcase into the graphic to represent a broken JPEG in 2012. Around when I came out as non-binary in the fall of 2019, I realized, in retrospect, that this refusal to dress up either as anything remotely masculine or feminine for so long was a tell.

So, in some sense, I owe Halloween and its insistence on pretending—as Vonnegut famously wrote, we are what we pretend to be—for an early piece of reassurance, as I grappled with whether I qualified as "queer enough" in the months surrounding my coming out. When I realized that I'd never taken the opportunity to dress up either as a man or as a woman over the course of the past nearly two decades' worth of Halloweens, it felt like a sign, something I could point to. The best kind of proof of all, one that extended deep into the past, back to before I knew what being non-binary was, before I'd ever heard or read the words. Proof that it was a descriptor, a shorthand for understanding something about me, rather than a buzzwordy trend I was hopping on.

/

I lied earlier. I did dress up a third time, sort of. I went as the colour grey in university—matching American Apparel hoodie and skinny jeans—to a Halloween party a few blocks from my place stuffed with other members of the creative writing program. One of those nights that I can recollect a dozen scenes from, all these years later. Wanting to write a short story about it at some point afterward. It came out as a few lines in a poem draft:

> We are chunked up in the haze of the basement, the house's fitting id.
> Over the din, Mario and Luigi are holding forth with a fireman. Tonight,
> I am nobody, so it's fitting that I'm talking to the well-dressed ghost of
> Allen Ginsberg. In the next room, a bedappled Eve is conspiring with the
> blue sky to pull off a ménage à trois under a rubicund cloud of Jell-O shots.

Something about this jumbled-together collection of such different ideas and images felt beautiful. The idea of a person being subsumed into their costume, at least for a few hours. Why had it been possible to be present then and so impossible to even make it out of my apartment every other year? There had been joy as that STM Metro card—a bus driver had let me ride for free, beautiful strangers in line outside a showing of *Rocky Horror* had asked for a photo with me. And though almost no one got the broken JPEG, that in and of itself was kind of apt.

But the fear response I felt every year was real. The rustle of excited voices a few blocks over, in every direction. That chaos. The association I always seem to have with unruliness in public—of unchecked male behaviour, anarchy, that I'm not safe. A cortisol spike that I cannot seem to will myself to push through. Unless I was doing it for love.

On some level, then, so much of the fear of Halloween was really a fear of men—what they could, might, would do when unshackled by the invisible web of rules that seemed to make up society the other 364 days a year. Whether they were lying in wait under piles of leaves, or hastening across the street to accost me. Or just laughing and yelling in the distance, breaking things—bottles, or rules, or laws. Maybe next year I'll host a Halloween party for some friends. Not having to go out—that could be the thing that saves me.

It is how my last name begins with the word *man.* How I will always have been born into this world with a penis between my legs and "Man-" on my birth certificate. A reversal of that internet meme about toy dinosaurs. *And yet a trace of the false self / exists in the true self.* It is crying when the intersex character in the teen TV show finds love. Thrilling to the music video of a beautiful man fronting an emo band, drawing *Xes* on his hands. Feeling my brain's jaw drop out of its mouth when a trans woman's perfect *n+1* essay so neatly draws the line between wanting to be a woman and wanting to kiss women. It is being misgendered by old friends, being misgendered by people who met me long after I came out, being misgendered in work emails at my day job and professionally as an author in Instagram posts celebrating me, or by a government-funded literary organization. It is running into a friend I've known for almost fifteen years. Her dog barking at me. She joking, "Good girl—thank you for always protecting me from strange men." My heart soundlessly breaking. For having thought I was neither strange nor man. But.

November

I FINALLY DELETED MY TWITTER ACCOUNT late in the summer of 2023, in August, around the time that India landed a rover on the moon, Justin and Sophie Grégoire Trudeau announced their separation, and the seventy-eighth anniversary of the Americans bombing Hiroshima and Nagasaki was observed.

Beyond the obvious reasons—that, as a microblogging platform, Twitter had always been a somewhat frivolous use of one's time; that it had also become, over the course of the past decade, a thoroughly toxic environment that rewarded, in ways big and small, cruelty, vitriol, and smirking condescension; that it had, since being bought by a particularly noxious South African billionaire in 2022, also become a noticeably worse version of itself, and seemed to be finding new ways to worsen even further by the day—I had a very personal reason to leave it behind for good. Which was: the death threats.

It wasn't the first time I had been the recipient of death threats online (nor, I fear, will it be the last), but the experience—a meme I posted going too viral, being encountered far outside of its original context and leading to mass vitriol—felt so emblematic of what was wrong with Twitter in the first place that it felt like an almost welcome excuse to give it up, a sort of embarrassing incident bringing to light a bad habit of mine that was past its best-before date, some form of digital rock bottom.

The fact that it wasn't my first go-round with death threats was interesting, because I was both somewhat inured to them and also triggered by them simultaneously, a hardened scar on my psyche that still throbbed when touched. My first go-round with online vitriol and harassment from strangers had been twelve years earlier, during my second of three years working as an editor at my alma mater's student newspaper, though the inciting incident, an article I'd written, preceded the first actual death threat response by several years. Because, after the initial wave of comments and messages died down, like some kind of horror movie villain, the issue would crop up again every year—during the month of November.

/

Originally, I'd wanted to call the piece "No-vember."

In retrospect, that detail was a fairly good tell that I was a neurodivergent twenty-three-year-old with a relative paucity of life experience and not someone whose opinions should have been paid much attention by the general public.

"Get it? It's like Movember, but, 'No'-vember."

"I'm just not sure that will be obvious to people," another editor had said, and it ran instead as the terse yet clear "No to Movember," with an accompanying illustration (childish in style, I felt) of a man trying to rip his own moustache off.

In the days between my writing the first draft of the piece (in an inspired flurry of typing during a Wednesday evening editorial meeting, when I should have been paying attention to the plans my fellow editors were hashing out for the upcoming issue) and its publication (six days later, on the first Tuesday of November 2011), I felt good about it.

After being asked to pen rough drafts of our editorials on student politics a handful of times, I'd gotten the hang, I thought, of writing opinion pieces for the paper I worked for, a free student weekly that ran out of a spacious, dingy office on the sixth floor of my university's Hall Building—named after a donor whose last name was capital-*H* Hall, not for the presence of a lower-case-*h* hall therein, as I'd realize many years into my undergraduate degree, though it did contain a large auditorium you'd be forgiven for mistaking for its titular hall.

I was the copy editor at the time, a position of vanishingly little prestige at a publication, but the role belied my textual chops. As my two-year stint in the position progressed, I came to take on what felt like a hybrid role, sort of like an athlete whose unique skill set allows them to rewrite the rules of a position, not quite a centre or a point guard, not quite a forward or a defenceman, but a rover.

Though a copy editor's job is nominally to spot the little mistakes others miss, the typos and style errors, the other editors at the paper increasingly relied on me for heavy lifting with pieces that "needed some love," and the editor-in-chief, a former graphics editor turned managing editor, freely acknowledged to me that she wouldn't have been able to do the job if not for the safety net of my editing skills.

I saw myself as someone with the sheer willpower and editorial chops to wrangle the frequently underwhelming or scattershot pieces of copy we were given by the unpaid students who did the bulk of the newspaper's writing. Maybe it was the years I'd spent reading magazine essays at my corner-store job, shift in and shift out, maybe it was being the eldest child of an editor / technical writer and a translator. Maybe it was growing up without a TV in the home and spending all my free time reading. Whatever it was, improving other people's writing felt like some sort of a calling, and dropping into a Word document that contained obvious textual missteps felt like a flow state to me.

The ways that other editors came to rely on my eye for finding and replacing awkward phrases and invented idioms was perhaps part of the problem, ultimately. Maybe I seemed more like someone who had a grip on working for a newspaper than I really did, a fraud passing too well until they're asked to do something they genuinely can't, Homer Simpson in the cockpit of a plane. The majority of the rest of masthead had some experience in the university's journalism program; they were being taught in concrete ways the basics of a series of procedures and ethics that I had only been able to intuit from a distance, a kind of Plato's cave of the student press.

In the space of a half-hour during that Wednesday meeting, I let a thought fall out of me and onto the computer screen to the tune of maybe seven hundred words: Why was Movember the charitable cause du jour—on campus and, seemingly, everywhere—when it only benefited men? And, from what I could tell, First World men at that, as the statistics at the time indicated prostate cancer was less of an issue in less prosperous countries.

Like many young leftists in my university cohort, I had learned about male privilege at some point in the prior year or two, and I had found it a powerful and compelling way of framing the events that made up the world around me. In this new context, the unfairness of everyone spending attention and money on what I now recognized—and had the terms to define—as a subset of the world's most privileged group of people jarred my twenty-three-year-old brain. What about all the people in the world suffering from diseases or horrible twists of fate who *hadn't* started by winning the global lottery? Here was something to rail against—I would open my fellow students' eyes to the contradiction of it all. We do not live in a vacuum, I thought; sad as it is, white men in North America getting prostate cancer was less sad than, for instance, children being born into abject poverty in the Global South. That seemed to my younger self like an obvious moral equation that would be hard to dispute.

In retrospect, it should have been obvious that was not the case. After submission, the piece received more pushback than I was used to at the paper, in that one of the two editorial passes specifically asked for the injection of statistics to back up my points. As someone who was, then and now, spiritually closer to a poet than a hard news reporter, threading my writing through with facts and citations was not my strong point. I preferred to gesture toward truths that I held in my head and that, especially at the time, I assumed the reader must, as well. I poked around online for data on prostate cancer for perhaps a half-hour, dropped a handful of facts in, and sent it back for a final edit, my own stance unchanged, and the piece's not much so.

You're reading this well over a decade later, so with the benefit of hindsight, you might be able to tell, by this point in the piece, that my screed was not well received. The vast majority of the response, of course, hinged on one crucial detail: Like any print publication worth its salt in 2011, my student paper had started uploading its articles online. At the time, as we wound down production, typically around 1 or 2 a.m. Tuesday morning, one member of the team would copy and paste the articles one by one into a low-rent CMS, set to go live a few hours later. That night, whoever uploaded the articles was unwittingly playing a major role in the future of my life.

/

The post that finally got me chased off Twitter in 2023 was a strange one. Before I posted it, I knew it had "the juice"—poster-speak for an innate online quality that would lead to engagement—but I couldn't imagine how powerful it would end up being. Because it was going to boast a Photoshopped image that would slot it into the context of an ongoing meme, I recall estimating that it might garner something like one hundred or two hundred likes. For me, those kinds of numbers were a rare win, something that might happen once a year or so. But it was also a very traditionally "me" post—couched in semantic layers rather than straightforward, a kind of metapost that was ultimately more about something personal than the eye-catching graphic it came wrapped in. As it happened, its eventual success was a combination of the two factors: It had one foot in a crowd-pleasing visual straightforwardness, and one foot in a kind of niche self-referentiality. In other words, like its subject matter, it was a hybrid of two styles.

The post I'm talking about was a Barbenheimer meme, a genre of post that existed for a few months that summer that mashed up the visual and thematic sensibilities of the two blockbuster movies released on July 21, 2023: *Barbie* and *Oppenheimer*. One was a movie glamorizing a highly destructive product of twentieth-century American global hegemonic power, and the other was a biopic about J. Robert Oppenheimer. I'm kidding, of course, mostly, but that was what was funny, for a moment, about the Barbenheimer phenomenon: the juxtaposition of such seemingly radically opposite stories allowed us to find unexpected parallels between them. It was an opportunity to think about Hollywood, the narratives it deems fit to bestow its outsize budgets upon, the great American mythmaking machine. It was also just an opportunity to get some jokes off.

In July of that summer, midway between an improvised solo *Past Lives / Asteroid City* double bill at the Forum, a movie theatre operating in the shell of the city's once-great cathedral to professional hockey, I was talking with my father. I had an hour to kill between movies, and he lives only a few minutes away from the movie theatre, so I texted him to see if he was free for a quick catch-up chat. As we sat on a bench near his place talking about movies, I realized I had to explain what Barbenheimer was to him. He took to the concept with an unexpected savant quality, a kind of outsider artist. As I went on to quote him in the eventual viral tweet: "What if you photoshopped a mushroom cloud so it looked like Barbie's hair? I bet that would go viral."

I didn't have the heart to tell him that it almost certainly wouldn't. I'd been on Twitter, sporadically at first and then with regularity as it picked up steam as a platform, since the beginning of 2009. I'd posted many thousands of times, and only one of them had ever gone genuinely viral, a post about ordering pizza online I made in August of 2016. It felt like trying to explain to a child that, statistically, a lottery ticket was just a worthless scrap of paper. But of course, the difference is that sometimes the numbers actually do hit.

My poster's instinct did tell me that there was something to his idea, and I had always liked tinkering with things in Photoshop. So a few days later, I did as he'd suggested—edited a picture of a mushroom cloud to look like it was Margot Robbie's hair. I tightened the aspect ratio so it wasn't quite as wide, which, to my father's intuition, made it a strikingly believable silhouette of mid-century housewife hair. I grabbed someone else's pink Barbenheimer logotype and slapped it on top. Then I added some copy in the text portion of the tweet: the context of me explaining Barbenheimer to my dad and his response, ending it with the pandering phrase "one like = one agreeing with my dad." I hit Send—around 11:30 p.m., much later than I would usually post anything that I hoped would garner attention—and went to bed.

/

The next day was a difficult one. The backlash did not, as online ones sometimes do, take any time to get started. It was fourteen years ago now, so I don't remember who first told me, but I was made aware at some point during the day that the article's comments section had blown up. Most of our pieces received no comments at all; this one already featured many dozens of comments, strangers calling me a bad person, a terrible writer. I skimmed through them. In the mix, I found the friends and roommates of our photo editor, guys I knew of but hadn't met, trashing the piece. Mocking a picture of me taken at a recent Friendsgiving party, in which an uninspiring patchwork of facial hair sat on my face. There, above my lips, a moustache of my own. A symbol of my seeming hypocrisy. There was a sense of the closeness of that, that these were guys I stood a decent chance of running into in a social situation. Who now found me monstrous, idiotic, reprehensible, worth publicly mocking on the internet.

The shock at having people only a few social degrees removed from me attacking me and the piece was unpleasant, but so was the reality that so many strangers were weighing in on the horribleness of it, too. This was a new experience, both for me and for the other editors. Though it had been founded in 1980, the paper had gained a website only recently, and the process of posting all its published content was essentially in its infancy. The idea that something written by and for the students of the university would be of interest to people who didn't live in Montreal and weren't currently attending a post-secondary institution was not on our minds. I'd made the mistake of thinking we were writing only for the university community. I was, I think, prepared for the piece to ruffle some feathers among my fellow students. But as the coming decade and change would make plain, any sufficiently inflammatory piece of writing, posted by any publication that seems to gesture at its own seriousness, will find its own worst audience. Water finds its level.

Over the course of the week, I was contacted by radio stations asking if I wanted to discuss the piece. I declined. I wanted to die, or at least to bury myself under something. What was wrong with me? I wondered. One of Canada's foremost magazines, *Maclean's*, published a piece on what I'd written and the response to it. It would remain at or near the top of the Google search results when you searched my name for years afterward.

In the immediate aftermath, it felt like my life ground to a stop, though somehow, I managed to keep showing up to work and school and newspaper meetings. I had a lot of time for soul-searching. Did I really hate men that badly? What had men ever done to me, growing up? I had seen uncles of mine behave boorishly. I had read stories, seen movies, with male villains. I had been lightly bullied by boys in school—mistreated but not really abused. At times, I had felt that my father loved me a little bit less than my mother did, because communicating true feelings was harder for him than it was for her, though in retrospect, likely much easier than it was for many of my peers' fathers. But what was I? Heartless? To brashly argue that prostate cancer was not a cause worth caring about when there were other problems in the world? I had applied a zero-sum logic to the money we give to charity. I had imagined each dollar going to the nebulous cause of curing prostate cancer taking food and clean water out of the mouths of the starving. I had been self-righteous about an issue I knew little about, either emotionally or intellectually.

The worst feeling, perhaps, was realizing that the other members of the paper didn't even take my side. That the opinions editor had strongly disagreed with my take, but had run the piece out of a sense of duty to include perspectives she didn't agree with. That the news editor was furious we'd run something so offensive without his realizing it. I asked the editor I had a crush on whether I was out of line. "I think you wanted to provoke," she said. I wondered how true that was.

/

The Barbenheimer tweet already had around two hundred likes by the time I woke up, and within a few hours that number had doubled. By the early afternoon, with the likes and retweets not slowing, I realized the weird alchemy I'd managed seven years earlier with a tweet about my pizza-ordering preferences was recurring. *Twin Peaks* It is happening again dot GIF. I was going genuinely viral.

The following week was a fun and strange one. After all the experiences with Movember-related attacks, I was primed to expect blowback whenever too many people encountered me or my writing online, but this experience of going viral felt surprisingly free of animus. People seemed genuinely jazzed—primarily by my dad's clever idea more than my execution of it, but also by the idea of a parent and child co-creating a self-fulfilling prophecy of a viral meme. We had asked for virality, and the internet, charmed by the frankness of the request, had granted it. The responses were wholesome. One guy even replied, misgendering me, then saw my pronouns in my bio and followed up to apologize and correct himself.

The initial wave of attention was followed, as it always is online, by knock-on effects. The post began to be featured in roundup articles. Searching for the copy, I found that other people had reposted it verbatim without credit. The Google Alert I have for my name turned up a fascinating new phenomenon: websites selling the tweet's graphic printed on T-shirts, seemingly set up to scrape the internet for any sufficiently viral image and then monetize it on the quick and dirty. The official *Barbie* movie Twitter account even responded to the tweet.

That seemed like the end of the good times to me, sort of like when Charli XCX tweeted "kamala IS brat" a summer later. Their response was written in the movie-specific phrasing of the tagline—"This Ken is a stylist"—and something about it didn't sit right with me. It wasn't clear to me whether they meant me or my father; if the former, they were misgendering me. Either way, the idea of either of us being a hairstylist in the context where Barbie's hair was a mushroom cloud felt. Off. In forcing me to think more about the reality of the image I'd produced, they brought up some of the unpleasantness that lay at its core.

Then the whole thing exploded.

/

For an article I had spent all of half an hour writing the first draft of, the piece had a shocking amount of staying power.

Long after the initial furor had died down, after I had published an official apology in the following week's paper, after we had devoted an entire page to sharing the angry letters to the editor it had provoked, after the editor-in-chief and the opinions editor had issued their own mea culpas, after one crotchety customer at the corner store I worked at had stopped mentioning the controversy during his regular visits, after my life had more or less gone back to normal, the months went by and then the calendar rolled back around to fall again, the following year. Thus began a kind of sick tradition: Every November for many, many years afterward, people would find and share the piece on Twitter or Reddit, a wave of angry online discourse would follow, and then I would be subjected to more hate-filled messages.

There was no way of knowing how intense a particular year's outburst would be, only that it was more likely to happen than not. So each October, as the days got shorter and colder, I would start to brace myself, and then take the month of November off Twitter. Some years I simply avoided posting anything; some I only replied to friends' tweets. Some years I logged off for the whole month, got my partner to change my password for me.

For an emotionally sensitive person, it was a logical response to the tension of wondering how much anger I would have to bear the brunt of this year. I remember things. That one terminally online Malaysian poster of ill repute stoking his followers' anger at me six or seven years after the fact. Someone in the tweets saying: "I think his apology was sincere." I still remember that to this day. A little drop of mercy in the sea of roiling outrage. But no one else agreed. The month of November still felt deeply haunted through my late twenties. Everything as of daylight savings time, frankly. The increased darkness. Feeling a kind of wickedness come over the world. Sensing angry men plotting against me. Though they never really did. But they still did things. My sister got Facebook messages. "I'm going to come to Montreal and kill your brother." The bizarre sexism in that, trying to scare her for having the audacity to be born to the same parents as me, about two and a half years later, as if she'd had a choice. The feeling, before that, of terror at the possibility of those I cared about finding out, of changing their minds. My father, whose older brother had beaten cancer, or my ex, or anyone whose respect I craved. Did my grandparents know? What would they think of me now? A freelancer at my job mentioning the fiasco to my boss after hearing of my employment. Somehow without consequence. Years later, a barrage of emails to my boss's boss demanding I be fired. Thankfully the instinct to close ranks. Circle the wagons rather than appease the mob. A stray tweet at some point in the early 2020s: "Are you *that* Alex Manley? The college newspaper one?"

At some point, the *Maclean's* article about me was no longer at the top of the Google hits when I searched for myself, as I too often did. The relief of that. Though what was a national newsmagazine doing publishing content about an article in a college paper? The way culture war shit leads to these pile-ons. *Can you believe what this misguided young person had the temerity to say in print? And that none of the other young people they worked with were wise enough to head it off at the pass?* As if any of the readers would ever read a single other article published by that particular university paper. It opened my eyes to the power of the world to correct you for being wrong about something. Not that I think I was, at least not in the way I was being told I was. Not in a way that merited death threats, or at least wishes for me to get cancer. Which I may still. Though the irony there: *In order to correct you for not thinking cancer is serious enough, I, who know how serious cancer is, wish it upon you.* The vast majority of online discourse is only slightly more serious than playground fights. This is human interaction for so many—dominance and submission, the libidinal economy, quick flights of rage before cooling down. So much of it by men, if we're being honest.

/

The official *Barbie* movie Twitter account weighing in—it had also responded to various other viral Barbenheimer tweets—was what finally pulled back the curtains on the unpleasantness underneath. Japanese Twitter caught wind of what was hot across the Pacific Ocean, and they were shocked at how callous we were being. By virtue of now being one of the most popular iterations of a Barbenheimer meme, my post was among those at the forefront. A screenshot of it was included in a petition that garnered tens of thousands of signatures. I was being asked, in my DMs, to consider various world historical tragedies happening to me. There was, I deciphered using Google Translate, at least one death threat, and some more death suggestions beyond that. The one that stuck with me the most was someone photoshopping a Barbie doll holding a machine gun in front of the Polytechnique memorial erected in Montreal to honour the fourteen women killed in a gender-based school shooting in 1992. *Not so funny now, is it?* The juxtaposition of these two radically different scales of tragedy, of a wartime act with a peacetime mass murder, belied the fact that that was what I had been doing originally too: manipulating pixels for online attention in a way that now felt all too close to dancing on the graves of the dead. All this from someone who'd seen neither movie (they weren't out yet when I posted the tweet), who'd never felt any particularly positive feelings toward Barbie dolls, who'd always regarded militaries, and the American military in particular, with distrust. Somehow, I felt, I had accidentally become a propagandist for a variety of things I disagreed with and had briefly been celebrated for it, and now the chickens were coming home to roost.

Someone emailed me to tell me I should apologize. But I knew that all I was capable of was throwing a towel over the flames. Online, you've got to deprive these things of oxygen. I deleted the tweet, and some others I'd made referencing the fact that I'd gone viral. And then, after a period, I deleted my account, ending my fifteen years on a platform that had made it seem funny—good, in fact—to make light of all those deaths. Even if that hadn't been how I, or seemingly anyone else in the first week that it was travelling around the globe, thought about it, even if it initially felt like I was just mashing up the most obvious visual signifiers of two different movies. It was an oversight on my part, but also on the part of all the people who'd crowed about the cleverness of the gag, and that felt weird. Why hadn't anyone said anything in the first act? How had we let these signifiers of mass death become neutral images, sapped of their grim power? Unlike the radioactivity itself, the images' effects had faded. At least on one side of the Pacific.

/

If student newspapers are indeed training grounds for careers in journalism, the Movember piece experience was actually quite salient: I got my first taste of a kind of online behaviour that would come to define an era of digital publishing in the decade to come. Over time, there came to be a name for what had happened to me: stochastic terrorism. The attempt to make someone feel fear via the internet, the manipulation of a stranger's cortisol via words and images.

In the years after 2011, how many writers for newspapers and magazines—essayists, columnists, reporters, interviewers, and more—would go on to taste the fury of the mob, for placing their names in pixelated proximity to an idea, sensible or otherwise, that displeased a particular group of people online (the right, more often than not) in the decade to come? How many emailed or Facebook Messengered insults and threats? How many attempts to get people fired or punished at work, in some cases successfully? How many people doxxed? Swatted? At a certain point it simply became part of the ecosystem. I spent the intervening years studiously avoiding opportunities to stir up the wrath of the mob, but still managed to feel a terror in the pit of my gut resurfacing every time I published any writing of any kind anywhere that strangers might see it, from online book reviews to print personal essays to tweets espousing something adjacent to an opinion. I became, at the behest of people who disagreed with even the views I could defend, anodyne and milquetoast, a sanded-down version of myself.

I still kept writing, kept trying to publish things, kept trying to be the self I had been following like a lodestar, but it was an odd experience. For a time, rejections always prompted paranoid wonderings. *Is this because of the Movember thing?* Trying to keep tabs on my own career for a long time felt dangerous, too. The bilious, bubbling shame of coming across the words "alex manley apology" as a suggested Google search—the stain on me, that felt like it would never wash off entirely, however faint it got over time. It's strange, how things live online.

But in early 2024, now on relatively comfortable terms with the process of searching for my own name online, I came across a new blog post excoriating me for what I'd written—penned by a man himself diagnosed with cancer. It was genuinely hard to imagine a student newspaper article continuing to hold such power over twelve years after it was published. The post's author accused me of hating men (true, at the time) and argued that my article was indicative of the kind of anti-male sentiment that caused men to avoid going to the doctor to get checked for things like prostate cancer in the first place. This felt less accurate, to me. I had not been expressing at the time, nor have I ever believed, the sentiment that men need to "toughen up" and do things like "push through the pain." I was angry at men because I didn't want to be one, and I was funnelling that deep, unspoken feeling through a new-found moral framework into an opinion piece for a school newspaper staffed almost exclusively by early-twentysomethings with fairly leftist politics. Was it possible that men who encountered the piece felt disheartened by it and came away from the experience less likely to be proactive about their prostate health, or any other aspect of their well-being? From behind the veil of my pain, I'd assumed they'd all see that the comments were unanimous in their rejection of my world view. I'd assumed they'd come across a screenshot of the piece on Reddit and joined in the melee with everyone else who hated my guts. I'd like to believe that my misguided screed didn't have any actual real-world effects, that it was just an opportunity for me to suffer at the hands of people who vocally felt that I didn't respect men enough. But I can't know for sure.

I considered sending him a message, pointing to the chapters in my last book, my guidebook for young men, where I explicitly advocate for them taking their health seriously, physical and mental. Writing these things never felt like penance for the Movember article, just a logically consistent position that I would expect anyone of conscience to hold. But would my trying to contradict his anger do him any good? Was I more valuable as a villain, was trying to clear my name just egotism? I couldn't settle on an answer. I never reached out.

Do I regret what I wrote? Of course I do. How could I not? The excerpted phrase that I have seen quoted most often, "prostate cancer is a hallmark of male privilege" is so insane it's hard to wrap my mind around, now. Who was the person who wrote those words? What I was trying to say was: "You can't get prostate cancer unless you're a man, and if you're a man, you experience male privilege, so should you really complain about it?" Even aside from the binaristic framing—my eliding of trans and non-binary people from the equation—this too is a self-evidently insane question. But I understand why my younger self felt it important to express. I had never had any meaningful experience of cancer, had not yet felt its capacity to lick, like flames, at the self, the family, the community. I had spent the past few years raging about men, and their toxic presence felt like a miasma I couldn't escape from. The two things weighed on me in vastly different ways, and at twenty-three, I found one heavier than the other.

Paradoxically, coming out as non-binary at thirty-one was the biggest single step in terms of my rapprochement with men. Unburdened from the shackles of feeling like something I wasn't, I could now approach men, both as people and as a concept, in a whole new way. One major upshot was that I found I hated them a lot less. Though my feelings of kinship with women and genderqueer people still took emotional precedence, I could see that men, too, were hurting, the ways in which men, too, were victims of patriarchal ideology, the ways in which men, too, often felt like imperfect fits within the context of an unbelievably restrictive modern view of masculinity.

As a non-binary person, I felt my love and appreciation for the best of men grow and blossom. I felt like I could now appreciate the aspects of manhood that I had taken for granted growing up—camaraderie, physicality, boisterousness. At long last, I was coming around to the beauty of "dudes rock."

It was in this context that I recognized, at some point, that much of the animus that came across in the Movember piece was simply my younger self's gender dysphoria mapped onto an attempt at a moral argument. Framing your feelings as a logical argument is rarely a winning proposition. In a different publication, my flailing arguments would never have seen the light of day; at the student paper, they skated through the editorial defences with relative ease.

Many years later, I came to better understand why the photo editor's roommates had come after me in the comments. In retrospect, of course they would. One of them—the angriest one—his father had died of this same cancer whose severity I had belittled. A pain I would never be able to understand, my own father having lived through my twenties and seemingly in good health midway through my thirties. I had never had to face growing up with a hole there. And here was my little shit article, pressing on the wound. Exposing how little I knew of the world, of life, of death. His sister, daughter of the same father, five years later praised my poetry collection. I wondered if she knew.

/

The Barbenheimer experience played out not unlike the Movember one—it hurt, a lot, at first. I spent a lot of time soul-searching, feeling the searing pain of finding myself the object of other people's anger.

Then, over time, the pain lessened. I felt myself coming back to myself, having learned something—about myself, about sharing things online, about how the internet works. Though so many things around these instances of outrage felt hot to the touch, impossible to go near, I finally got around to reading the seminal text about my experiences: Jon Ronson's book *So You've Been Publicly Shamed.*

In it, I came across a quote by Mike Hubacek, who killed two people in a drunk-driving accident in 1996 as a teen: "It's a part of me. I suffered a lot of survivor's guilt. At the time, I almost convinced myself I was in a living purgatory. I lived to suffer." Then a line that grounds the feeling: "I went more than a year and a half without looking in a mirror. You learn to shave using your hand as a guide."[25] It, too, is a type of poem.

Ronson doesn't spend much time on it, but he does briefly address the core questions at stake when discussing disgraced pop science writer Jonah Lehrer—was the person at the centre of the online maelstrom a public figure, or a private individual?

Some of the question of how much I deserved it must have been riding on what people saw me as—whether they indeed saw me as a public figure or not. In the period after the Movember article came out, though I did have a masthead position, it was at a student paper. I was very much not a public figure, so much so that I was barely an outside-my-apartment figure. The

25 Jon Ronson, *So You've Been Publicly Shamed* (Riverhead Books, 2015).

second time, first as tragedy then as farce, I was a thirty-four-year-old with a few thousand Twitter followers, a media job, and a book out.

Either way, Ronson's book seems to have trouble articulating a position on shame, other than that it is powerful. I think about cancel culture, how important it is, how bad it is, how necessary it is, how illusory it is. To have twice set off such different groups of people, on the back of such different types of online content—was it a skill? Or a curse? What was wrong with me? I wondered. Was it some aspect of my neurodivergence? Had I been raised wrong? Was there a secret heartlessness at the core of me? Or was it just a feature of what the modern internet was like? If you stick your neck out just far enough, just often enough.

/

I wonder sometimes who I would have turned out to be had the Movember piece never seen the light of day. What kind of writer, what kind of thinker, what kind of citizen of the internet. Would I be a better version of me, less afraid to speak my mind, more confident in my beliefs and the voicing thereof? Would I have been someone who strove to be a "thought leader"? To speak out in defence of those hard done by, to build momentum for progressive movements? Would I have been someone with more than 1,500-odd Instagram followers, who believed in themself and what was right, who could handle pushback?

More likely, I imagine, I would have continued on being angry at men until some other platform gave me the opportunity to voice my displeasure. I could have written the kind of performative personal essay that would have set media Twitter on fire for a few hours in the early 2010s, become the proverbial main character for a day, instantly making a name for myself as the punchline to a series of overly online jokes, provoking an even more powerful and lasting anxiety. Maybe that would have made me give up writing for good—who knows. That's the funny thing about wishing the past were different—it might always have been worse, instead of better.

It is feeling so much more myself as out, but still never knowing quite how to be. It is seeing online, over and over, that non-binary people don't owe anyone androgyny, while still feeling myself to be in endless, unrepayable androgyny debt. Considering filing for androgyny bankruptcy. It is telling my grandmother, having her accept me, then her forgetting, introducing me as grandson again in conversation. It is nail polish staying on until it's gone, because taking it off myself after decades of not wearing it (high school experiments with Liquid Paper notwithstanding) feels wrong, and I'm so bad still at applying it, putting off my next sloppy attempt. It is learning on Instagram how many other cultures have had non-binary conceptions of gender throughout history, how many societies constricted into the black-and-whiteness of man/woman by colonial forces in the past few centuries.

The Content Mines

OF COURSE WE CALLED IT THAT—at least a handful of times. How could we not?

We knew how frivolous our jobs seemed, how puny and pathetic our on-the-clock efforts were, compared to our ancestors' and forebears', how little physical effort we expended—so little that we needed to play soccer on our lunch hours during the summer just to break a sweat. Then back to our desks to spend a few more hours trawling the internet in the air conditioning.

It was days spent overhearing Kevin and Franz taking extended breaks to play foosball in the kitchen. Tom always with his long phone conversations that the rest of us had to listen in on with his twenty-year-old girlfriend, seventeen or eighteen years his junior. The half-full bottles of liquor on more desks than they weren't. The PowerPoint presentations—always the PowerPoint presentations, which had indeed started to be called slide decks by the end. The Habs season tickets and free items of swag that continually filtered through the office. The beer fridge that appeared at some point in the dev section, stocked with Budweisers and Goose Islands. Though by then, by virtue of having copy-edited an article on seasonal winter beers early on in my time there, I knew I only liked the maltier stuff.

But yes. Of course we called it that, at least on occasion. It was a common self-deprecating jab for people working in digital publishing at the time: *Another day down in the content mines.* Our browsers pickaxes, our keyboards tools for refining the raw ore we came across. Scanning every stray bit of text to see if it could be turned into traffic. A viral airplane breakup. A couple having sex in a parking lot. Celebrity nudes leaked en masse. What was the digital publishing version of black lung? Where, or what, was our canary?

/

I got the job in a way that no longer exists: I applied via Craigslist, had one interview (in-person), did a short editing and writing test after it, and then was hired on the spot ("Are you free to come in on Monday?").

Though it was preceded by an anxious summer spent working on a heavily Tao Lin–inspired autofictional novel and avoiding the reality of my financial situation, the fact that it was my literal first interview out of undergrad makes it all the more egregious; though this was only 2013, at times I feel like a millennial version of the boomer reminiscing about buying a house with a union job salary and nothing more than a high school diploma.

I remember a few things from before I got the job—my best friend worrying that the other employees, the *men*, would eat me alive, or something to that effect; the fact that I came across the job listing on Facebook when a school friend posted about it in a contemptuous, mocking way ("Can you imagine me leaving school to make $40,000 a year copy editing for a men's website?") and, having just graduated, feeling keenly the six or so thousand dollars of student debt I carried, thought, "Okay, but that would actually be pretty close to perfect"; the anxiety I felt about buying a new, office-friendly shirt and pair of pants at the downtown H&M just for the interview, knowing I hadn't worked since January and it was already early August, and how much would I regret these purchases if I didn't get the job. Maybe, I thought, I could use them again for the next job interview I did, somewhere else. Though there wouldn't be a next interview. Not in person, anyway, not since, not ever.

The first few months were part-time, in-office, freelance work. I was writing and copy-editing, skittering around the edges of everyone else, trying not to make too much noise lest someone notice me, notice I didn't belong. Like when the co-founder GM ran into me in the entranceway and asked me what

I did there, and then, musing on the concept of copy editing, told me to my face that they'd A/B tested articles that had and hadn't been copy edited and there was no measurable difference in how they performed. Besides the casual cruelty of the top boss telling a new employee their job is completely meaningless, he was, of course, being prescient. The position of copy editor would largely cease to exist within a decade, and most of those jobs were gone within two or three years of his comment.

But my value to the company quickly became a question of finding other kinds of mistakes than mere typographical ones. My literal first day on the job there was an emergency all-hands meeting to address a Jezebel piece decrying the site as a haven of sexist bullshit; I was tasked, not long afterward, with going through the archives and classifying top-performing articles as either keep, rewrite, or delete on the merits of how misogynistic they were in both content and form. It was an approach and a task that would come to define the majority of my work for the following decade—covering up the site's egregiously sexist back catalogue and replacing it with something palatable to the site's modern, forward-thinking readers, a group of people, I would come to understand in the years to come, who barely existed.

After a month and a half or so, the impending liability I'd been brought in as a backup plan to cover for came due—the existing copy editor lost her battle to extend her work visa and had to return to the States. I found out like this: One day she stood up and yelled "Fuck!" really loudly from her desk a few cubicles away. "Language," Dave, her neighbour, chided her. "They're kicking me out of the country," she replied. "Oh," he said. I knew then, in that moment, what it meant—that I was getting her job. It was, at that point of my life at least, certainly the clearest example of a singular moment where someone else's loss was my gain, someone else's suffering my profit, the zero sum game of office politics.

Only a few months after conceiving of the job hunt as insurmountable, infinite, oceanic—in a note I'd written to myself about how to end my novel, where I suggested comparing the relentless updating of Craigslist as akin to Gurov and Anna watching the sea roll in and out at the end of Chekhov's "The Lady with the Dog" ("So it must have sounded when there was no Yalta, no Oreanda here; so it sounds now, and it will sound as indifferently and monotonously when we are all no more."[26])—I was going to have a job, a real-deal job. Health insurance, retirement funds, the whole thing.

26 Anton Chekhov, "The Lady With the Dog," trans. Constance Garnett, *Fiction 100: An Anthology of Short Fiction*, ed. James Pickering, 11th edition (Prentice-Hall, 2007).

/

In many ways, the job was a dream job. When they finally brought me in full-time a month or so after that fateful "Fuck!," they offered me the old copy editor's salary: $43,676, well over the $40,000 I was expecting to encounter, the bottom end of the range that had been posted on Craigslist. I had never made more than about $10,000 a year previously. Roughly quadrupling my salary overnight was life changing. The office was located in Montreal's artsy Plateau-Mont-Royal neighbourhood, on the eighth floor of a thirteen-storey office building at the intersection of two main streets. Delicious lunch options abounded nearby, though a careful accounting of my spending habits will reveal I significantly over-relied on Subway and Thai Express in the early going.

After a month or so, the photo editor, who'd started only a few months before me, revealed that he, too, was a recent alum of his university's left-wing student paper. We bonded, and a friend group with some of the other younger employees sprang up in the years to come. The job also produced a steady stream of surprising experiences: a Johnnie Walker Scotch tasting at my boss's home, press trips to Phoenix, Vegas, and Philadelphia, and free stuff: assorted articles of clothing, a free pair of ludicrous limited edition candy-red Timberlands, a bottle of Glenlivet. Every summer, there was Spa Day, when the staff retreated to nearby Mont-Tremblant for a morning at an expensive Scandinavian nature spa and an open-bar afternoon at a lakefront beach club. We even drank mimosas on the rented bus. At times, working there felt like being part of an exclusive club as much as it felt like having a job.

Other stories stuck with me—the apocryphal tale of the time they'd been shipped a giant box full of Fleshlights, which had been left in the darkened video room and, like a tin of forbidden sweets, had slowly dwindled in secret until there were none left. The polar opposite of what I imagine must happen when a women's publication gets a box of sex toys—a bunch of men shamefully grabbing a handful of pleasure and skulking off. And the founding myth of the site: that a group of guys who wanted to start a business had noticed a man wearing white socks with a suit in a café and thought there should be a resource to tell guys not to do that. Though, a snarky voice in the back of my head says, *Caring about another man's outfit? How gay is that?* The co-founder who had stuck around long enough to be the GM in the first few years I was there dressed quite well and was always clean shaven and well groomed. But maybe it's just that he was European.

As I realized after years on the job, the concept of a men's magazine can always be turned back around in on itself a little. Sure, men might be manly. But magazines, ultimately, are inherently effeminate enterprises, temples to the value of the written word, teamwork, perfectionism, and aesthetics. None of the guys I worked with were especially macho; they were chauvinistic and curt and brash and terse and managed like emotionally distant fathers, but they would not have been able to win any kind of lumberjack or strongman competitions. And by the end of it all, the women on staff—who were competent, efficient, and hard-working—had started to become managers, two female co-workers of mine promoted over me despite having less experience, in no small part because, whatever my talents for writing and editing, I could not meet a deadline to save my life.

/

It was a turbulent time to work in digital media, which is to say, it was *a* time to work in digital media, an industry that had never been particularly stable. Facebook was still clinging to its big lie about its video play metrics, which meant that I was watching the BuzzFeed watermelon stream live at work, waiting for it to burst along with everyone else. There was the endless sexual tension between us and social traffic. Other publishers were crushing it, even in our space, so why couldn't we? A typical article shared to our page would often garner single-digit likes, along with a comment or two deriding us for not being manly enough. Meanwhile, a British men's site called UNILAD had viral Facebook video hits every week, buying the rights to stuff that seemed like it would hit and reaping the traffic. (Though in retrospect, after Facebook's video metrics were revealed to be largely fictional, that may have been a waste of money.)

Eight months after I was hired, one of my fellow editors became our first-ever news editor in a bid to capitalize on the explosion of "quick-hit" social- and search-driven online news content. For the next few years, we became content miners—his job, and to a degree all of the team's, now involved trawling the internet for nuggets of raw content and polishing them just so for clickability and audience engagement. It was a bit of trial and error, seeing what hit and what didn't—articles about porn stars, poker stars, viral social media trends, press releases from dating apps, studies showing something about masculinity, new trailers for movie sequels we thought would appeal.

Though my role in all this was indistinct in the early going, one of the first tasks I was given outside of the basic scope of editing copy was a headline analysis. I took to it with aplomb, scoping out hundreds of headlines at competing websites—BuzzFeed, Gawker, Elite Daily, Upworthy—to try and reverse-engineer their respective approaches. Before long, I was pumping headlines out in fluent headlinese, in step with everyone else on the internet in the mid-2010s. It was just a particular way of writing, and I was a writer, after all. The Flashiest Player In Hockey Is Also One Of The Flashiest Dressers. Last Night Was Amazing And You Know It, But Is She Worth Going All In? The 20 Craziest Supercars We've Ever Wished We Could Drive. Watch Urban Freestyle Skiers Land Some Of The Craziest Jumps in the Middle Of A Ski Resort. We Sent A Writer To Phoenix To Train Like an NFL Prospect. He Survived. Barely. 1 Extreme Urban Skier + 1 GoPro + A Pinch Of Danger = 1 Seriously Awesome Video. If Video Games Get Any More Realistic Than This … (This Clip Will Blow You Away).

/

Of course my best friend had been right to be anxious. I wasn't eaten alive by the place, though in the early years, as the copy editor, I developed a habit of leaving around midnight on Fridays, swamped by the job of having to copy-edit three days' worth of content in a single workday at the end of each week. But unpleasant things did happen, as they do at every workplace, and especially ones that are male-dominated. Besides the ways in which I felt awkward, on edge, and perpetually on the verge of being fired, the other employees were not great about the newly emerging discourse around transness. I had to argue fervently against the publication of transphobic content—a personal essay about a Thai sex worker, an iffy framing of Chelsea Manning in a separate editorial feature. One day, the video team's casual office conversation in the open-concept space turned to the topic of trans people. I don't remember a single thing that was said, only the mix of callous humour and disdain that came through in their voices. Pretty quickly, overhearing what they had to say became so painful that I had to leave the office entirely. I went for a walk around the floor so my breathing and heart rate could return to sea level. I wouldn't come out as non-binary for another half decade or so.

Then, late in my tenure there, a more senior co-worker—the brother of one of the co-founders—slapped my ass as we passed each other in the doorway to the lunchroom. He'd been teasing me with what felt like increasingly uncomfortable familiarity for a while. Ass slaps are one of those things, in male culture, that are hard to quantify. If you slap a stranger's ass without warning, it's light sexual assault. If you slap your buddy's ass without warning, you're probably just on a baseball team together. When I got back to my desk I messaged my new manager about the incident. "I don't want him to get in trouble," I said, "but I want this on the record in case he tries anything else." I didn't like how it felt; it had crossed a line.

Then I messaged him and told him not to do it again. Considering the white-hot, shouting rage he expressed when I had laughingly accused him, a huge *Star Wars* fan, of sexism for finding *Star Wars*–branded makeup ridiculous but not, well, every other *Star Wars*–branded product in the world, he took it well. He never touched me again. Left me alone pretty much completely. Which was nice. But I wonder how things went for the women who worked there over the years, when they received unwanted attention from men in the office. How gender, or perceived gender, would have factored into the response. I knew that race didn't, at least during my tenure; during the five years I worked in that office, I never worked with a single woman of colour at the company.

This is part of the problem with start-ups and small businesses—they are always at the whim of the thoughts and feelings of a small group of people who may not have much experience managing, and company culture flows from the top. In digital publishing, as in many other tech and tech-adjacent workplaces, a certain lawlessness can be seen as a feature, not a bug. Things like guardrails, checks and balances—these will only slow you down, they fear. And they certainly wouldn't fit in with the casual boys' club vibe.

/

What kind of masculinity were we peddling, exactly, working at a men's site? It *was* regressive, at times, especially in the early going, but rarely egregiously. It wasn't especially progressive either, though. Like much of North American masculinity in the 2010s, more than anything, it was confused, a mixture of an inertial, slowly eroding corpus of twentieth-century manhood and a sense that things *had*, in fact, changed—without any clear grasp of the new boundaries or guidelines, and no prophets to pass them on down from the mount.

Ultimately, I think, the site's masculinity was a sort that was friendly to advertisers above all else. Where there were ad dollars, we followed. At one point the site started up a Latino-themed offshoot, headed up by an incredibly non-Hispanic white guy, specifically to court a perceived wealth of ad spend money for the demographic that was, as yet, underserved on the editorial front. It was a different time, of course, and some of this was just leftovers from the fact that the site was a product of the dot-com boom, a nineties kid that hadn't yet pivoted to the staunch identity politics of the Trump era. It had nothing to cast itself against; it was just free-floating in a sea of slowly disappearing search traffic and increasingly programmatic ad revenue.

Of course, the men in the office's occasionally visibly retrograde politics weren't just at odds with my secret queer neurodivergent snowflakiness, they also felt out of step with the bloodless corporate vision the sales team had for the site. That conception, as far as I could tell, was a slick, professional-looking, highly marketable website that gestured toward the symbols and signs of masculinity without actually engaging in the kind of grunginess that guys actually seemed to appreciate. As ever, the real enemy of masculine identity wasn't women or femininity, it was capitalism. However much it seemed like a distinctly male ideology, eventually I realized there was no bastion of toughness or machismo or bravado that the money men wouldn't sell out for a few bucks or a better margin.

The motto was on the wall at the front: "Become a Better Man." But it was empty. Underneath the words, there was, for a time, an unused reception desk, and then later, a fake plant. There was no real guiding ethos, no belief in the capacity of men to do good, no burgeoning conception of a healthy masculinity. Whatever the Facebook comments accused us of believing when it came to feminism, the most anti-man aspect of the place was how hollow it all felt. It was dress shirts, nice colognes, expensive booze, feet up on the desk, shooting the shit.

/

In the fall of 2018, following a stretch of several months of significantly decreased productivity on my part—my executive function always craters after a breakup—I was unceremoniously shuffled out of my position as a full-time employee. Two managerial types based in New York City offered me the option to go freelance, and then, when I turned it down, made it clear that it was not so much a choice as a demand. If I opted to stay, they said, they would use the fact that a "performance improvement plan" had been opened to help get me back on track by a manager who left over the summer to pull a fast one, radically hike the amount of work I had to do, and then immediately fire me if I so much as failed to meet a single deadline. This was the *HR works for management, not you* truism in a nutshell. I typed up a letter to announce that I was quitting, feeling like nothing so much as a hostage reading the kidnappers' script. Just like that, I was no longer an employee of the digital publishing industry.

With the benefit of hindsight, I can see that we were right, in a way, about our jobs being in the content mines. It was an accidentally apt comparison, not because of the sheer perfection of the inversion—that working in a mine is exactly as hard as typing away at a laptop in an air-conditioned room is easy—but because ultimately, both jobs are slivers of history: time-stamps of a particular era, each a boom tied to a new kind of technology, each just waiting to become anachronistic, joke fodder for future generations of workers. Like coal miners, or whale oil hunters, we worked with ragtag groups of people in similar circumstances to ours; as we worked, friendships and relationships were born and died off. Like coal miners, or whale oil hunters, we were all just loose numbers in the giant math equation of capital. Like coal miners, or whale oil hunters, we were using up our youth extracting a resource that, for a moment in time, was capable of making other, older people, people we'd never met and never would, rich.

And then, eventually, it wasn't. In early 2019, not long after the end of my first go-round at the site, I visited the office I'd recently stopped calling home for five days a week, a sort of phantom limb not far from the foot of Mount Royal. The trend had been well underway the year before, but in my absence, Suite 801 had turned into another thing we associate with the resource extraction industry and its centuries of greed: a ghost town.

You build up the infrastructure to allow for money-making, you create spaces where your workers can be human beings, as workers are so often wont to do, and when the flow in the money pipe starts petering out, you move on. So often, the infrastructure remains, telling a new story to those who encounter it, reminding them that industry is a fickle enterprise.

What had once been a buzzing office of thirty to forty employees, replete with all the trappings of a real workplace—managers, departments, HR, a real corner office, a panini press in the kitchen, meeting rooms with silly names that gestured toward a company culture; in short, a genuinely bustling place—had been reduced to an embarrassment, something that was almost hard to look at. Now, seven or eight people were clustered in one corner, set up at row desks without dividers between them, the office's cubicles sold off for scraps, or, more likely, carted away by a private junk removal company.

Even that wouldn't last. Before the pandemic ripped through the remaining vestiges of North American office culture the following year, at some point in 2019, the whole publication's physical footprint—which once boasted multi-employee offices in four countries on three different continents—had been replaced by a subscription to a single WeWork in downtown Montreal.

I never bothered going to check the WeWork out, though they invited me to join them. As someone with a deep-seated forever fear of being socially excluded, I appreciated the offer, on some level, but the prospect of announcing in advance that I'd be popping by for a few hours of work felt weird, no less so because who would really *want* to visit a WeWork?

/

A video on the would-be YouTube replacement Nebula teaches me about contemporary coal mining. Shifting economic, technological, and material realities have drastically altered its practice; the version that occurs in the twenty-first century is almost unrecognizable. Gone are the pickaxes; human beings barely factor into matters. Most of the coal extraction in North America happens in strip mines close to the surface, rather than the deeper ones from the nineteenth and twentieth centuries. Giant extractive machines now make their way through these spaces, chewing up all in front of them. A human in protective gear stands nearby, making sure nothing goes wrong. *How fitting,* I think. The content mines version of this is not hard to conjure: A team of writers and editors replaced by a single person in charge of a fully automated production process: SEO content, optimized H2 section heads, AI slop for copy and lead images, algorithmically scheduled posts. Everything streamlined, robotic, impossible to romanticize.

/

Credit to the managerial types, after I went through the rigamarole of quitting, they did continue to give me a good amount of freelance work—initially, enough to cover more than my old salary, though I no longer had benefits or stability. However, without any concrete obligations to me, it was an amount that slowly decreased until it was about half of what I'd been making. But when economic headwinds (COVID-19) slashed freelance budgets at publications worldwide sixteen months later, my former employer was no different. My income plummeted even further.

Paradoxically, except for one single month in the summer of 2020, it was never low enough to meet the qualifications for the Canada Emergency

Response Benefit, but was still much lower than that of people whose incomes had been reduced to nothing, and who thus did qualify for CERB. Luckily, a freelance editing gig working on a retired children's singer-songwriter's memoir about his mental health struggles, then an unexpected sojourn into the world of literary translation, then a CCA grant to help write *The New Masculinity*, my last book, helped keep me afloat until the spring of 2022.

That's when the editor who had replaced me at my old job let me know he was moving on. I sent an email to his new boss inquiring about returning to my former position. As it happened, the managerial types based in New York whose favour I had lost were no longer in the mix, and the hiring manager was looking for someone with experience in the field.

I thought about the way the site felt now, nearly a decade after I was hired, how many articles were genuinely progressive, how much of the cruft of sexist schlock had been deleted or rewritten. At times over the years, people had told me that what I'd done at the place was something to be proud of, a compliment I was always quick to brush aside. Though the traffic numbers showed otherwise, it always felt like no one read these articles, really, at least not anyone I knew, and before I came out, the work had not infrequently felt like a Sisyphean exercise in gender guilt, trying to undo the harm that men had done. Now, for a brief period, I contemplated the possibility that I actually had changed something for the better.

It almost felt like an uplifting story a progressive publication might have written about in the heady early days of content mining. This Young Employee Sought to Change a Media Company From Within—What Happened Next Is Shocking. A Heartwarming Story: This Gender Ally Helped Make a Men's Publication WAY More Feminist. Diversity Win? "Cishet White Man" Hired by Men's Website Turns Out to Actually Be Bisexual Non-Binary Person! This LGBTQ+ Hero Helped Turn a Long-Time Bastion of the Manosphere Into a Refreshingly Progressive Online Presence. 9 Years Later, You Won't Believe What This Regressive "Men's Site" Looks Like Today.

This time, I did have to go through the updated interview process: the phone pre-interview, the Zoom interview, the content plan PDF. They let me skip the writing sample portion of the process based on the fact that, well, I'd written several hundred articles for the company already. A few weeks later, I'd gotten the job back, and my boomer luck kicked in yet another time—they offered me $10,000 a year more than I'd asked for. What can I say? I strapped my helmet on, turned on the headlamp, and climbed back down into the mines.

It is trying to draw on wings before nights out, anxious and worried about running late, smudging, uneven. It is trying to figure out when to be quiet and when to be vocal about misgendering. And how my decisions will impact how the next non-binary person is treated. It is the way they pronouns make me plural, or unknowable, or both. It is the way I don't want a man body or a woman body, I want a *Paul Takes the Form of a Mortal Girl* by Andrea Lawlor body. Changeability. The ability to change. It is the writer Daniel Lavery asking his Twitter followers—before he was out, before he was going by Daniel—to sum their genders up in one GIF. Me, years before coming out, knowing something was up but not how to say it, sharing a moment from *Princess Mononoke.* San and Ashitaka fighting with blades. A clash between a sad boy and an angry girl. There are two wolves inside you.

The Rat's Tale

I MUST HAVE BEEN ABOUT SEVEN YEARS OLD when, sitting in the chair at the women's hair salon on Boulevard De Maisonneuve in Westmount, I asked the stylist to leave a little spot longer at the back.

My mother would take me there for periodic haircuts for many years, though there was a barbershop next door. Still, in the feminine confines of the salon, I only ever opted for a straight buzz cut. On this particular occasion, though, something sparked in me. Adrift in the black leather chair and plastic cloak, I made a choice. I didn't even know the words, then, for what I wanted—the short, two-syllable phrase so universally disdained: *rat tail*. All I knew was that I wanted it.

The request was the Saint-Henri boys' fault. Not that they pressured me into it; though we shared the same neighbourhood, we spoke different languages and rarely interacted, if ever. Rather, they were a shimmering presence at the corner of my eye, southwest of nearby Station Lionel-Groulx, a group I was aware of and afraid of in equal measure. To an outsider, they may not have looked much different than me. We were both, after all, on the wrong side of the tracks. But to a shy, bookish, lonely anglophone growing up in one of the poorest neighbourhoods in 1990s separatism–frenzied Montreal, they were everything my younger self was not: self-assured, powerful, numerous, authentic, and capital-*F* Francophone.

They probably came from working-class backgrounds, as I did, though my parents both had liberal arts bachelor's degrees. They probably grew up, as I did, in modest homes, maybe got by, as my family had, without a car, and maybe made do, as we had, without brand new clothes or brand-name shoes or a microwave in the kitchen. Maybe one or two of them, like me, even lived in a home without a television, though my parents' choice to forgo the living-room staple was an ideological one, not a penny-pinching technique.

Unlike me, however, because they most likely spoke better French than English, the Saint-Henri boys' worlds would have been circumscribed by the steep hill you had to climb if you wanted to get from our neighbourhood to the bright lights and bustle of downtown, or to the well-groomed, tree-lined avenues of Westmount. If Montreal was truly the Paris of North America, then its French-speaking poor to the south, east, and north of its centre were the denizens of the *banlieues*. They may have fit into our neighbourhood better than I did, but their ability to move through the city's moneyed nucleus, with its glass skyscrapers and office jobs, and comfortable west end, with its well-groomed lawns, was dictated not only by education and peer networks but by being able to speak the lingua franca of the rest of the continent.

As a shy kid with undiagnosed anxiety issues, most of my youth felt like a game of cat and mouse: Selfhood was less a question of authentically pursuing my own desires and more a question of saying yes to the right opportunity at the right time. It would be decades before I started making more confident decisions about my life, whether the choice was a job or a haircut. All I knew then was I'd seen the Saint-Henri boys with rat tails, they looked different in a cool way I wasn't then able to articulate, and a group of that size surely couldn't be wrong about something like that. So I made my request to the hairdresser, a shaky declaration of agency, a step toward the making of the self.

/

A year or so later, my family moved north to lower Westmount in a surprising feat of upward mobility. My father's employer had gone public and offered stock options to its employees; my parents cashed them in and moved us into a beautiful ground-floor condo on cozy Grosvenor Avenue. I cried when they replaced our long-suffering floral-patterned couch, its frame covered in streaks of marker and battle scars inflicted by the cat we used to have. But, in retrospect, it wasn't very Westmount.

Though my new address was only a four-minute Metro ride from the Saint-Henri bubble, the two felt universes apart, separated by a steep hill and the proverbial tracks we used to live on the wrong side of. Whereas in Saint-Henri I'd been an awkward anglophone in a sea of francophony, in Westmount I was still a loner—a comparatively poor kid interloping among the wealthy, from the scions of Montreal dynasties to the merely well-off. Always, I was bookish, nerdy, effeminate, and socially inept. And still, the rat tail continued to grow. I kept it on at successive haircut appointments, perhaps wanting to prove that I was still, even tenuously, Alex from the block, tied to my working-class roots by those swirling brown strands of rebellion.

But as it grew, so too did the volume of insults it attracted. My new classmates seemed to have a name for it before I did, a phrase that made the rounds like a bad joke or an urban legend. *Rat tail.* The least appetizing part of the least likeable animal. Where had they all come across this knowledge? While watching television, maybe, or while hanging out with friends? In any case, each person also seemed to have come to the same conclusion: My rat tail was bad.

Yet I wore it for years, alone in the quest of it. Why did I keep it, weathering the insults and embarrassment, the hundreds of times someone must have looked at me and thought I was cute until they caught sight of the tail? Why keep it, when the world kept telling me to shear it off? It might just have started out as a refusal to admit I was wrong, the way children can be stubborn. Gradually, though, it became a physical manifestation of something more important: my ever-present feeling of being an outsider. At the time, I only understood this sensation in very personal terms. It made sense to me that my hair should also set me apart, warding off normies and welcoming weirdos. But, as the years passed, I came to understand how both class and gender were layered into the feeling—though, as I'd also learn, these readings can be contradictory.

/

As I'd intuited young, haircuts are signifiers of style and selfhood: Punks get mohawks, army recruits get buzz cuts. Butches go short, femmes go long. Office workers get No. 2s; fashionistas get high 'n' tights; young children, before it makes sense to spend money on their looks, get bowl cuts. Many haircuts are objectively ridiculous: the fade, the devilock, the trihawk, the one where the barber buzzes a swoosh into the side of the head, the obnoxious cuts that famous rockers like Chad Kroeger or Deryck Whibley sported, the Flock of Seagulls, the comb-over. But haircuts are also context-specific, taking their meaning from the community that sees them and what they perceive as stylish or meaningful. In some cultures, boys might see long hair as a symbol of virility, haircuts as emblematic of castration. Growing your hair might be a religious duty, a sign of both obeisance and belonging. In other cases, the opposite will be true—long hair a sign of effeminacy, weakness, indulgence compared to the compact masculinity of the buzz cut, the crew cut.

My mistake, it seemed, was transporting a mullet-adjacent haircut whose coolness was legible in one space—working-class, French-speaking Saint-Henri—up the hill to posh, stuffy anglophone Westmount. Living where I was, I felt an innate, unspoken understanding that the haircut was Bad because it was a Low-Class Haircut, though the teasing was rarely directly along class lines and more often about gender, the way my last name diverged from the vibes I gave off so starkly. Students nicknamed me Alex Girly, Alex Womanly, Alex Not-So-Manly. People suggested I cut it off, lest they do it for me. In daydreams, I dodged a crew of scissor-wielding popular kids intent on a violence that, then and now, felt radically out of step with the severity of the offence, the kids who'd threatened that my ass would be grass if I tried to upstage them at the Grade 6 talent show by performing the chess-themed parody version of "S Club Party" that I'd written lyrics to, printed out, and shown to a friend, who'd shown them to a friend, and word had gotten around, the way it does among twelve-year-olds, high on their burgeoning understanding of social hierarchies and the powers of shame and clout.

The rat tail—unlike so many well-known haircuts that are proudly worn by given members of a culture or subculture, looks passed down like heirlooms—is something of an orphan, a bastard son of a thousand fathers, claimed by no one, a cultural failure, a flop. On Urban Dictionary it's ascribed, variously and crudely, to rednecks, Germans, and Hispanics or the children of eighties and nineties "gangster parents."[27] Google's Ngram feature shows usage for the term spiking significantly in the 1940s and staying steadily popular ever since.

The website Hairstyle Camp, meanwhile, suggests rat tails are most popular in Australia and New Zealand and that, despite not being mainstream, they

27 "Rat-Tail," Urban Dictionary, archived April 26, 2021, at https://web.archive.org/web/20210426054244/https://www.urbandictionary.com/define.php?term=RAT%20TAIL&page=3.

are "making a comeback."[28] The site offers the discerning browser twenty different variations on the rat-tail style, from the elaborate (chignon, fishtail braid) to the classic (curly tail, single curl) to the ill-advised (one variant called "rat splat" makes the titular critter all too explicit). The photo evidence appears evenly split between professional soccer players in action, hair-salon glamour shots, and anonymous photos of unsuspecting children sitting in classrooms.

It's this latter category that seems to dominate public perception; the rat tail is a haircut doomed to be surreptitiously photographed and mocked. It bespeaks no special talent on the part of the hairdresser and can easily be done on the cheap, if not for free. The lone Urban Dictionary description that verges on positive pegs it, a little desperately, as "one of the few hair styles that is still truly individualist"; the entry has 105 downvotes to only fifty upvotes, by far the worst ratio on the page.[29] When celebrities give it a whirl, like the since-disgraced Shia LaBeouf did in 2015 for his role in *American Honey*, it's often met with peanut-gallery laughter. Though a few men's fashion sites responded with how-to content, one pest-control company offered the star $10,000 to cut it off as a PR stunt.[30] They, like my schoolyard tormentors, couldn't help but insist, *That thing needs to go*.

Even my partner, upon seeing the photograph on the Wikipedia page for the rat tail, expressed her revulsion despite my just having said, "Honestly, this looks like it could have been me in the nineties." In addition to its class signification, the gendered aspect to the rat tail—a lock of long, lustrous femininity breaking through the masculine crop—affects how the style and its wearers are perceived. That it mixes together two nominally opposite, even competing gendered understandings of hair means it lives in a kind of nether zone. On the one hand, it's a haircut associated with a certain version of white American masculinity—LaBeouf's, for instance, was thick, braided, and tied off at the end with a rubber band, tough and terse. But on me, a skinny nerd with no pretensions to machismo, my wispy rat tail's more effeminate qualities were much more pronounced.

/

28 "25 Hottest Rat Tail Hairstyles for 2021," Hairstyle Camp, archived June 7, 2021, at https://web.archive.org/web/20210507071956/https://hairstylecamp.com/rat-tail-hair/.

29 "Rat-Tail."

30 Ann Oldenburg, "Terminix Offers Shia LaBeouf $10,000 to Cut off his Rattail," *USA Today*, March 9, 2015, https://www.usatoday.com/story/life/entertainthis/2015/03/09/terminix-offers-shia-labeouf-10000-to-cut-off-his-rattail/77489664/.

I hadn't thought it possible, but by the start of high school, the anti–rat tail sentiment had intensified from the middling disgust my hair aroused in elementary school. Faced with a new crop of students and no longer among the school's eldest, I was easily placed on the bottommost rung of the pecking order.

The school was located in Montreal West, a sleepy suburb twenty minutes west, on the other side of Notre-Dame-de-Grâce from Westmount, less wealthy than my home borough but not without its share of sizable houses, manicured lawns, and upper-class pretensions. I was still a year or two shy of my growth spurt and had no musculature to speak of. My social skills were still crawling out of the pubescent soup of my developing brain. I clung to the strands of my dignity and got the tail cut down to about half its length near the end of the school year, but that dignity was dwindling.

One night in early August of 2001, as I lay in bed trying to fall asleep, I found myself imagining the upcoming school year. I envisioned myself stoically trying to make it through another year of having no friends, hearing insults in computer class, feeling a jerk at the base of my skull as I stood reading something on a bulletin board and turning to find an older student laughing. Who the hell tugs a stranger's hair in the hallway?

My mind swelled up like a wave, forming a single, solitary sentence, the logical conclusion of a long, inexorable uphill march through the bullshit gateways society erects on behalf of the capitalist heteropatriarchy to exclude, sand down, disempower, and crush the spirits of people who don't conform:

If I have to go through another year of this, I'm going to kill myself.

I was six weeks shy of my thirteenth birthday. Propelled by a force of will I did not know myself to possess, I strode quickly to the bathroom. Before second thoughts or sentimentality could stop me, I dug my mother's scissors from a drawer and snipped off my rat tail at the spot where my spine met my skull.

My mother must have wandered in then, her parental intuition tingling, and she consoled me when she realized what had happened. We swept the hairs into an envelope and tucked the furry little corpse at the bottom of my chest of drawers. It stayed there until I moved out. I probably still have it somewhere, buried in some box full of other memories, childhood keepsakes still radiating slow and steady waves of sentiment as they make their way through their respective half-lives.

/

What didn't change, over the years, was that sense of being an outsider, a weirdo. After I came out as non-binary at thirty-one, my years-long willingness to hold fast to a haircut against the tide of public sentiment, a style for men that was tinged with female-coded flair that only a fear of dying could convince me to part with, finally clarified my younger self's persistence.

I thought about something my grade school friend Tadzeo had said: he'd advised me to keep it, said it made me unique. His words had made sense to me at the time, because when I wore the rat tail, it was as a badge of outsider pride, a sort of queerness avant la lettre. For many years after I moved to Westmount, I was the only person I knew or saw who had one. As I began to make my way in the world of social interactions, the spectre of the rat tail became little more than a skeleton in my closet, a childhood foible I hoped my high school friends wouldn't reveal to new acquaintances, though they often delighted in doing just that.

But I understand now that having the rat tail didn't single me out as anything so much as fashion-unconsciously poor. The tough kids I used to watch from a distance are making their way through a world much harder for them to move through than it was for me. If I'd really wanted, I could have just cut my hair and blended in, strands slipping from my neck to reveal a normal, middle-class white kid whose parents had managed to squirrel enough away to pay for a university education, a rat deserting a sinking class signifier.

The last time I saw something that looked like a rat tail online, it was in a meme claiming "When this haircut shows up in your Hood / it means your rent is about to increase," accompanied by four young white people rocking looks that meld TERF bangs in the front with, well, party in the back—a sort of rat tail / mullet hybrid that seems like middle-class kids winking at the cut's working-class connotations.[31]

Well-off white kids appropriating poverty is hardly new—something somewhat like that, after all, was what was going on when I got my rat tail—but the ease with which the haircut could become a symbol not of the poor but of those displacing them was jarring to me. But that's how style and class intermingle: a snake swallowing a rat gnawing at its own tail.

/

31 Shift_In_Emphasis, "Rule," Reddit, accessed March 14, 2025, https://www.reddit.com/r/196/comments/latvtv/rule/.

I was confronted, once again, by my childhood rat tail recently, sitting in a circle of people—friends, acquaintances, and strangers—at a baby shower being held at one of the city's more interesting bars. I had the misfortune of showing up late, slotting in directly between my partner and someone I'd been feeling a bit of a crush toward, a seating arrangement part rom-com and part sitcom. As an old friend of mine and I recounted how we'd met to my crush, my friend leaned in conspiratorially. *Alex used to have a rat tail, you know?* Here, again, the schoolyard feeling.

It is the photos of me with my childhood rat tail, its curling brown strands. It is a photo of me from a family vacation to Paris in 2004 that shows me in a black bowler hat, a royal-blue tank, and a green necklace. Something in my eyes exudes Alex from *A Clockwork Orange*. Something so *queer* about it. Maybe just my long eyelashes. But. It is pictures that find me giving in to an urge to express some femininity, couched as a joke—sporting a classmate's stereotypically feminine mid-2000s sunglasses at my high school science fair; again with women's sunglasses, this time holding tight to a friend's purse in an alleyway in 2007; waving a frilly pink umbrella around while walking to a friend's birthday party in 2009, a silk bandana tied around my head. In these photos, as in so many of me, my face seeming to alternate between shy and over-the-top playful, afraid to strike a pose but nonetheless finding myself doing so on frequent occasions. A love-hate relationship with attention. Coquettish.

I Grow Old, I Grow Old

What if guys went bald every fall like trees losing leaves but then it always grew back in the spring? Like trees?
—@smokeismedicine, Twitter

THE THOUGHT ONLY SEEMED TO COME IN THE MIRROR. It played out staccato like a chess game, tennis match, sword fight.

It's helping.

No, it's not.

It could be.

It's obviously not helping. Look, the spot there, a bit back from the front, to the left—no, the right—it's barer than before.

Okay. So maybe it's not helping—but if I wasn't doing it, it might be even worse than it is now.

I'm talking about the Rogaine. I'd been rubbing the foam into my scalp—nominally twice a day, though like any person with ADHD and anxiety, I'm far from perfect at remembering to complete my daily tasks—for about a year already. To address My Problem, which people who identify as men call "male pattern baldness." A tube that's supposed to last you a month costs about sixty dollars, but apparently no longer requires a prescription, as it did when I first started using it. I still can't tell you if it's helping or not.

Of course, it's embarrassing. Rogaine feels like such an awfully cishet man product to me. It speaks above all, I believe, to a male desire to be attractive to women, since they are so associated with thick heads of hair, with flowing locks. Is the gay community more comfortable with the image of the sexy bald man? The beefy-armed cue-ball chrome dome? Does seeing your own hair thin make you judge a potential romantic prospect's fading hairline more relatable or an image of disgust, vulnerable, taboo? In any case, as I began to seriously confront the fact that my hair was thinning a few years back, the question of how this affected me as a non-binary person arose alongside it.

/

My first act as a non-binary person, after all, was dyeing my hair pink. I made the decision before I'd even come out; it was a statement choice, and a photo of my new 'do was the exclamation point on the sentence. Along with the cut, the colour cost north of $250, a bracing welcome to the world of femininity via professional hair care. My days of $20 barbershop cuts while the men fought to see who could say more sexist things were over.

Though my gender does not line up with the sex I was assigned at birth, my experience with dysphoria and dysmorphia has been a bit all over the place. I quite like having a penis, though honestly I don't especially care for testicles. I don't mind being tall, but I do wish I were skinnier in a feminine way. I don't crave surgery, but I do wish I didn't have facial hair or body hair, and if I ever had the money I'd probably look into laser hair removal. I think male modes of dress are largely boring, but it's a boringness I feel comfortable in, and I have close to zero interest in wearing dresses or skirts. I'm curious about makeup, a little bit, but most of it feels overwhelming. I like the idea of earrings but haven't yet gotten the courage to pierce my ears, and after I lost one earring from my favourite pair of clip-ons, I've largely stopped wearing them. I wasn't someone who wanted to go on hormones; I had felt the faint pull of estrogen on a handful of occasions, but it never felt right for me, ultimately, didn't feel like the right magic spell for the changes I wanted for myself.

On some level, then, I understood that hair was the easiest, best, most fun place for me to express my gender. Since the pink, I've gone back to get it dyed silver, pink again, and, most recently, turquoise. Watching the colours fade over the first few weeks to a uniform blond and then watching the blond hold tight while my natural brown sprouts irrepressibly up below it has been fun. For a long, long time, all through my teens and twenties, my hair was a place of conformity, one that, on some level, I longed to use for exploring but didn't know how to bring myself to. Coming out finally allowed me to confront, to satisfy, that desire. It felt, well, affirming.

/

I first encountered T.S. Eliot's poem "The Love Song of J. Alfred Prufrock" in CEGEP, I think, the year after high school, but my most vivid memory is from a few years later, of reading it aloud to my then-girlfriend in the dry and empty wading pool in the neighbourhood park we had both played in as children, years apart. A September or October afternoon. Her studying it for the first time, like I had, in English class, the first year after high school.

It was the first time, perhaps, I had ever read a poem aloud in that kind of way—the way where you're trying, not consciously, but trying nonetheless on some level to bind yourself and the words and the other person together, three strands in a braid. The poem a jewel-rich vein running through the two of you. To speak something, beauty and meaning, into being.

I do remember something from when I studied it in class, though. Of reading and feeling a little shimmer, a little stutter, a little weakness, like biting down on something cold with too-tender teeth. The part about aging—one of my first memories of fearing it. I saw myself too well in the titular character, and these lines made some part of me wince.

> And indeed there will be time
> To wonder, "Do I dare?" and, "Do I dare?"
> Time to turn back and descend the stair,
> With a bald spot in the middle of my hair —
> (They will say: "How his hair is growing thin!")

Beyond this moment—beyond "How his hair is growing thin!"—I also encounter aging in other sentences that stick to me. I encounter books that say, "Time is a thing that the body moves through." PR emails in my inbox that say, "Rob Lowe on Feeling Lonely, Unheard and Unseen—The Radically Reframing Aging Summit." TV shows that say, "Death created time to grow the things that it would kill." Commercials that say, "Hey Richard, two minutes for looking so good." "Touch of Gray" by Just for Men and "Touch of Grey" by the Grateful Dead. While writing this piece, while compiling those quotes, I encountered another one in an unlikely source—the African American physicist Stephon Alexander's book, *Fear of a Black Universe*. Buried in the book's last chapter, it goes like this: "Wheeler believed that the universe implemented Darwinian evolution—and, as I and Salvador Almagro-Moreno argued, the entropocentric principle to create conscious life for the universe to observe itself."[32]

Let's try that again, simpler this time, like a pared-down riff, when the drums and bass drop out for a moment to let you focus on the melody:

the universe

implemented evolution

to observe itself.

Death created time to grow the things that it would kill. Life created time to grow the things that it would awe.

/

At some point, I wonder: *Surely, I can't be the first person in human history to dye their hair pink to obfuscate a growing bald spot.* And yet, there can't have been many of us. Pink hair dye wouldn't have been easy to produce for most of human existence on this planet. It wouldn't have been widely available until quite recently, the mid- to late-twentieth century. The Venn diagram of people dyeing their hair pink and people going bald would nearly be two separate circles. And of course not everyone has a roughly pink-coloured scalp. Not that that was the only, or even the main reason I was dyeing my hair pink. But it did feel like a slight reason to nudge it in that direction over turquoise and silver, my other two picks.

And yet I do have a special relationship with turquoise. I've had a thing for the colour for as long as I can remember. I don't think about it every day, or even every week. I don't live in an apartment covered in it. I'm not sure I even own a single item of genuinely turquoise clothing. But a special feeling of affinity for the colour has been a part of my life, a thread woven into it. A ribbon winding through it, a river, a ripple, like a more exciting flavour setting off the base one in a tub of ice cream.

32 Stephon Alexander, *Fear of a Black Universe: An Outsider's Guide to the Future of Physics* (Basic Books, 2021).

Partly it's because I associate the colour turquoise with attraction and seduction. I knew this fifteen years ago when I was working on my second novel project, a fiction manuscript that was heavy on wordplay and the overwrought dramatics of a twenty-year-old's emotional landscape and light on almost everything else. But one of the characters wore turquoise in a way that excited another character. So it was there, at least, fifteen years ago, and likely much longer.

I'm not sure where this association came from, exactly. My best guess is it stemmed from one of the outfits Jasmine wears in the 1992 *Aladdin*, which I would have seen, like most millennials, at least once at some point during the nineties, a decade I began in toddlerhood and ended in tweendom. Her impossibly lithe figure adorned with baggy turquoise pants. Sparking something in my younger self.

Perhaps the worst part of the feeling is that my brain produces a lot of false turquoise positives. But maybe that's only part of the appeal. It feels like a slippery colour to me, slippery and hard to pin down, neither one nor the other, one shade subducting under another, tectonic palettes. I pick up its ghostly presence in seafoams and mints, in aquas and teals, in certain greener sky blues. I like that it's a mix of two other colours, the most famous of the tertiary colours. Like me, something caught between two fixed points. I like that its name is simply the French word for "Turkish," a fact I found delicious enough to put into a novel I tried to write when I was in my mid-twenties, a decade ago.

> There was something to the word "Turkish"—the way it turned, like a turnkey, the slow, uninteresting "tur" into the collision with the "k," and the explosion billowing out, "ishhhh." Turquoise was different; the explosion was contained, muffled, like an explosion underwater experienced from the shore, but the initial "turk" was much the same.

I am not the only thing in the world with an affinity for this kind of hair colour. Is there anything, after all, more classic than a building with a turquoise roof? Oxidized copper domes gleaming in the sun. The stately reverence. With turquoise hair I could be such a building.

/

Of course, like everything else in the world, hair loss, too, has been subsumed into transness, at least somewhat, like how fresh ways of looking at reality allow for a new perspective on everything within it. One of the most beautiful things I've ever read is a sentence about being trans I saw on Twitter. It went something like, every person assigned male at birth has a potential breast size, and they'll never find out what it is unless they start taking hormones.

The idea that our bodies contain within them the blueprints for gender markers we do not claim as our own is a fascinating and unsounded depth of human thought, a beautiful, glittering pool whose bottom we have not yet attempted to touch.

Thomas Page McBee, for one, has at least done a jackknife dive into those waters. As he writes in his wrenching, gorgeous memoir, *Man Alive,*

> In more anxious moments, washing my hands in single-stall gas station johns, I hoped that being a man would not feel like pretending. I looked in the mirror and tried to imagine myself into being. I could have a deep voice or a reedy one, I could become bald or not, I could be skinny or muscular, hairy or pimply.
> I was a mystery to myself, and yet my body knew what it needed. My body waited for me.[33]

I wondered what that might be like, the idea of anticipating a baldness, of awaiting it like one might await a child, that your body failing you is somehow a sign of rightness, of success. It was a hopeful concept, but one I felt outside of. Did any older trans women rejoice to find out they could no longer achieve erections? At least going grey, and then white, was gender neutral. Even dogs do it, for that matter.

/

Still, when I wrote this essay in 2022, these questions remained as yet academic for what felt like the overwhelming majority of out trans and non-binary people. Though there wasn't a lot of data on the subject at the time—and isn't much more now—quite apart from the since-debunked factoid that trans women die on average at the age of thirty-five, the figures that are available suggest that trans and non-binary people, as a cohort, are younger than the

33 Thomas Page McBee, *Man Alive: A True Story of Violence, Forgiveness and Becoming a Man* (City Lights Publishers, 2014).

average population, largely because younger people come out at higher rates than older people. And with a growing acceptance of transness leading to children as young as five or six coming out in the past decade, it was plausible for me that the median age for trans people was actually dropping even as our numbers swelled. At thirty-three, when I first wrote this, I hardly qualified as an ancient trans person, but it often felt like I was over a decade removed from where the action was. Which meant, for better or for worse, that the embodied experiences I was living through were ones that most trans people hadn't encountered yet, and, in many cases, hadn't even begun to consider. And while many trans people will find themselves aching for a different kind of aging as they hit middle age, as their bodies begin to deteriorate and change in sexed ways that may feel like betrayals, then, and now, there is simply no playbook for aging in a non-binary body. It's a kind of freedom, of course, but also a form of aloneness.

/

When was the last time you saw a sexy bald woman? I don't mean a woman with her hair shaved close, like Amber Rose or *V for Vendetta*–era Natalie Portman. I mean a woman with a Mr. Clean–style cue-ball head—or worse, the inescapably male look that mixes sheer baldness on top with hair around the back and sides. Female sexiness is so wedded to thick hair flowing from the top of the head that it's conceptually hard to imagine without it. (You may remember the 2022 Oscars ceremony: the comic's wisecrack about a movie star's bald wife, the slap, the tape delay, the awkwardness that hung in the air, a kind of moral-clarity power vacuum. The discourses that sprang from it like Hydra heads.)

While the first signifier of beginning to go bald may be that one is moving away from youth, to begin to go bald is also to move inexorably away from femininity, from the possibility of expressing a feminine beauty.

For someone who was just coming into my appreciation, in a real way, of that potential in my own male-presenting body, that was a blow. I was only beginning, it felt like, to become myself, when genes, hormones, the inscrutable hard-coded logics of the body were already robbing me of the fullness of that self. I would never be the me I could have been.

Of course, no one is guaranteed beauty. We don't deserve it, we aren't promised it. That's sort of the point—it's more a measure of what some people have and most others don't than it is any one set of visual standards. We see that in the way ideals shift. People love to parrot that old saw that beauty is in the eye of the beholder, but what's more interesting about it is that certain time- and place-specific groups of beholders all seem to agree on a specific look, only for it to fall out of favour as soon as you cross a border, whether between countries or between decades.

So I think about wigs, another hallmark of trans life. They can make any kind of wig these days—they could make a wig that looks like the hair I wish I had—short and masculine in length, unmistakably feminine in colour. Do I have wig money? Do I have wig confidence? Do I have a certain wig je ne sais quoi? Would wearing a wig make me more like a sad businessman with a toupée or a drag queen? Would wearing a wig feel *non-binary* to me?

Of course, as the Twitter truism goes, non-binary people don't owe anyone androgyny. But that doesn't mean some of us don't feel like we do, don't feel—as bisexuals sometimes do—that we're not being "queer enough." Did I recently describe myself to a friend as "diet trans" for feeling like my transness wasn't "embodied" enough? I did. Do I feel guilty whenever I let my nail polish lapse? I do. And when an old friend offered to take me out to get my ears pierced and I took over half a year off to get back to her? It ate at me. How will I feel when it's too late for me, when the hole in the ozone layer of my hair grows too big to paper over and I need to embrace being bald?

/

Here's how I ended the original version of this piece: "I lied about the mirror earlier, actually. I also think about My Problem in summer, when I'm caught in an unexpected rain, fat droplets thinning my hair down to what feels like nothing, exposing the weak spots. Like I'm made of something sweet and sticky that dissolves in water. Spun sugar. Of course, no one is guaranteed beauty. We don't deserve it, we aren't promised it. But if you'll excuse me, I'm still in mourning for the body I wanted. I will never be the me I could have been."

Then, a tonal shift: "But I hope the next wave of non-binary kids gets to make the most out of their hair while they still have it. And with luck, maybe one day I'll be the older non-binary person a younger version of me sees as a model for aging gracefully."

/

Neither sentiment would end up being fully true, though. In early August 2023, I got an email linking to the online version of this essay, first published in *This Magazine* in 2022. A PR person was asking me if I would be interested in receiving an all-expenses-paid trip to Istanbul in order to receive a new kind of hair treatment. If I wanted Turkish hair transplant surgery. After a year of hemming and hawing and back-and-forth emails, I said yes.

/

I lied, earlier. I didn't encounter "Alfred Prufrock" for the first time in CEGEP, actually. Or rather, that was my first time reading the whole text, though it wasn't my first time being exposed to its essence. My father—who had been a poet in his youth and a technical writer for much of his adult life—once wrote a parody version, "The Love Song of J. Alfred Techrock," which I must have read somewhere when it was lying around the house. It began,

> Let us go then, you and I,
> While the design is
> being tweaked on the fly
> On a laptop Ethernetized with a cable;
> Let us go, through certain half-deserted halls,
> The muttering scope creeps
> Of broken code in nightly recompiles
> And stormy meetings with engineers:
> Specs that follow like a specious argument
> Of hideous extent
> To lead you to an overwhelming question …
> Oh, do not ask, "Will it ship?"
> Let us go and start a rumor.
>
> In the room the techies come and go
> Talking of the coming IPO.

The human brain is a beautiful thing, and there is tragedy in the fact that we insist so many minds spend so much time devoted to making so few people so much money. I think about things like this every time I hear people talking about traffic, real-life versions of that series of *SNL* "The Californians" skits. Life created time to grow the things that it would stick in gridlock.

It is to my father that I talk about baldness the summer before my trip to Turkey. He tells me something he has never told me before: He still has dreams where he has hair. A beautiful full head of hair. He looks at it in the mirror and combs it. And wakes up bald. It feels incredibly tender to see the sadness encapsulated in this story. How real the pain of going bald is for cis men, too.

/

So, in late October 2024, I boarded a Lufthansa flight to Frankfurt, where I'd have a two-hour layover before catching a second flight to Istanbul. There, a team of surgeons would remove hair follicles from the back of my head (the "donor area") and implant them into the top of it, in a six-hour procedure that would cause me so much blood loss that I'd almost faint. *Like a patient etherized upon a table.* And then, if everything went right, and I followed the complex aftercare procedures properly, after six to ten months, I wouldn't be balding anymore, my own follicles growing from my own head like little shoots, coming up in springtime, and I could dye the mass of them any colour I liked, and walk around in the rain without fear, and smile at attractive people that I met, knowing that I looked good, too.

And I felt strange about that, of course, scared and excited and also sad, sad that I had grabbed a life preserver not every person in my position could afford, knowing that trans people are less likely than cis people to have thousands to spare, even if gender-affirming surgery hardly counts as frivolous. Was I any different, or at least much different, from rich people getting Botox, thereby making wrinkles a defining feature of poor people's looks? Each one making the decision that made their lives much easier and others' lives infinitesimally harder. The way these things add up. An opaqueness of translucence. What of all the poor, balding non-binary people I had left behind? What about trying to forge a new path, a new way for non-binary people to look? What about my plans to be bald-headed but with a beautifully dyed beard instead? But I didn't have an answer for that.

It is

watching as friendships fall away and wondering if this is just the natural way of things or whether my new, complex gender played a role. Long-standing friendships with women whose subtle masculine leanings seemed to mirror my own femininities. When I came out, did I force them to confront a kind of conundrum, an unanswerable question about who they really were too? Our respective traits no longer in balance. It is a photo of me dressed head to toe in women's clothes from our family dress-up chest in the mid-nineties. At some point, when I found that photo as a twentysomething, being filled with shame. The utter humiliation of catching your younger self cross-dressing. The vulnerability of the way I didn't look embarrassed. That I was, instead, working it—or trying to. But I didn't tear the photo up, or burn it, or throw it out. I folded it in half, bending a guilty crease into the centre, and stuffed it back in a box somewhere. Leaving it for my future self to find. How at one point something had felt right about wearing women's clothes, about wrapping myself in beauty.

How to Come Out as Non-Binary If You're AMAB

THE PRECIPITATING EVENT WAS A BREAKUP EMAIL.

Not from a prior partner, but—possibly worse?—from a friend, someone I had counted as one of my closest for almost eight years. It arrived in my inbox in July of 2018, about fifteen months before the fateful Instagram post (pink hair, soft pose, paragraph caption) that did the job of explaining to the world (or at least to my followers) that I was coming out as non-binary.

Those eight years we'd been friends belied the fact that she—let's call her Jessie—hadn't been in touch as much since she'd moved to Toronto a few years prior. I'd been all too willing to make excuses for her, to subsist on twice-yearly get-togethers so long as they felt heartfelt and intimate in place of any kind of ongoing dialogue when her text responses always seemed to come hours later and the exchanges never lasted as long as they used to when we were in the same creative writing program.

For the time we were friends, I trusted Jessie's moral compass more than perhaps any other person's. She was my feminist hero, deeply and meaningfully intersectional long before her peers seemed to be.

So of course the friendship didn't last. Who would ever want to be someone else's high priest of feminism over eggs benedict and career / love-life updates twice a year? Her email, somewhere in the neighbourhood of a thousand words long, in response to a specific instance of hurt but detailing a pattern of smaller prior ones, precluded any possibility of a reconciliation. She accused me of using our friendship as a marker of my supposed trustworthiness, her name as passkey. She asked me not to reply, but instead to work on myself.

And I did—though not, I suppose, in ways either of us could have foreseen.

/

I'd mentioned aspects of my gender dysphoria to a few friends over the years and to my therapist, but it was always very tentative. I was just asking questions. How else to get at something so buried? I had internalized so much self-hatred because I knew I hated men and I felt like I was one of them. How could I not hate myself? Accepting that maybe I wasn't one felt like giving a pardon to someone who didn't deserve it.

The first person I did come out to was my partner. I had told her at some point—half a year before my Instagram post—about how weird gender was for me, and she'd been very understanding, but I wasn't sure how she'd take it as a public declaration of something, un-take-back-able. When I was ready to post about it, I told her in a food court, which feels psychotic, but we were about to go clothes shopping, which is such a gendered activity, and that felt right, somehow.

She was so supportive and loving, and that gave me the confidence to go through with it. I had drafted my Instagram post and then turned my phone to airplane mode to have the conversation with her. Afterward, I turned my data back on and posted the photo, turned it back to airplane mode, and tried to enjoy our outing without thinking about it. The social media equivalent of tossing a live grenade into a room and then closing the door. When I finally came back to Instagram, the comments were so supportive and loving and positive. Queer pals and acquaintances sent me DMs. I felt welcomed into something.

Of course, though my coming-out post itself was only in the works for a few weeks, and the heightened intensity of my introspection around gender was a year and change from the tectonic shocks of the summer of 2018, the road I took to coming out to myself was a deeply non-linear lifelong project.

As someone who spent many years denying to myself that I was really, actually non-binary before coming out as non-binary, looking back at the historical record and searching for clues has been a weakness of mine, a guilty pleasure to indulge in, running a tongue over a missing tooth. *Look*, I want to say. *Here's proof. I'm not making it up*. Moments in the vast digital archive of my life where I can see little traces of gender breaking through the mass of normativity, the moon shining through tree branches on a cold night.

Because, in some sense, I'd been pushed toward my coming out, there was always a voice in the back of my head telling me, *This isn't real. You're lying. You just want to be safe from their accusations, and this felt like the easiest way*. Like a certain Hollywood actor cynically coming out as gay, trying to get in front of abuse allegations. Like the way I worry when I'm leaving a store without buying something that I'll be accused of theft. Always feeling guilty for something. I think that's why the other part of my brain was so obsessed with scouring for proof. A kind of gender-based Gollum back-and-forth: "You're cis. You're a man. A hateful man." "N-no I'm not. I'm not. Look!"

/

I don't remember the first time I met Jessie, whether it was in the halls at school, or at an event, or online. I do remember the sense that I would hold throughout the eight years of our friendship—that she was special, more interesting than everyone else, a kind of celebrity, maybe.

By the summer of 2010, I remember knowing that she had come on board as the literary arts editor at the student paper I'd contributed to for most of the 2008–09 academic year. After being a regular presence for two semesters, primarily as a graphics contributor, contributing scanned pencil drawings to accompany articles, I ran for election as copy editor. I lost by a single vote in a tiebreaking round to an existing member of masthead, which I did not realize at the time was an incredible vote of confidence in me, not a door being slammed shut in my face.

Years later, after seeing incumbents easily beat out contributors every single time they faced each other for masthead elections, I realized to what degree my near-upset was an aberration. At the time, though, stung, I stopped coming by for production nights and took the 2009–10 academic year off from student newspapering. But when I heard that Jessie was the new lit editor, I felt drawn to return. Maybe there was a ... And we could be ... It'd be worth a shot, anyway.

In fact, my arrival for prod night on the first paper before the 2010 semester started was well timed; Jessie had actually quit a few days prior. I was pressed into service as the interim literary arts editor, officially voted in uncontested a few weeks later, and held the position until masthead elections the following spring, when I ran, this time successfully, for the copy editor position, as the literary arts section was folded into the larger arts section, no longer deemed worthy of a specialized section and masthead role. Though I had missed out on making a connection with Jessie in the student newspaper office, it was her absence, I now realize, that played a major role in my career journey, a kind of matchmaker in absentia. By taking the role and then backing out at the last minute, she left the team scrambling, and by unknowingly prompting me to show up, made me into a relatively uncomplicated replacement.

I don't remember whether I found out just before or just after, but I did see Jessie that week, just not on campus. Two days before the release of the issue that marked my return, she and a friend were moshing at a Titus Andronicus concert at Montreal's legendary Il Motore. I remember watching from a few metres away. Wondering if I could say hey or not. Never knowing how to be, around people. At the paper, I was told that she'd quit because her grandmother had died. I tried to square this knowledge with the image in my head, of her enraptured by the band's punky noise. Having such a one-note understanding of grief at the time. My own four grandparents all still alive. At least for the next few years.

My new-found role as literary arts editor was a boon not just to my career aspirations but also to my social ones; I now had an unavoidable reason to attend the literary arts events going on, all the excuse I needed to push through my social anxiety and start being part of the community in some meaningful way. Again, I don't remember when and how, but likely because I was going out more, Jessie and I started to become friends later that fall, and when she invited me out for beers in December, just the two of us, I felt like I had made it. It was the first time in my life anyone—a woman, especially—had asked me out for one-on-one beers.

/

I can pinpoint when transness became real to me. It was in 2010, in the person of a sweet boy I'll call James, who started writing a column for the college paper I'd just begun editing at. James used his column to educate the student body at the university about the realities of being trans. As the copy editor, I had the job of reading over every single column, so in a quite accidental way I had a front-row seat to a crash course in the ins and outs of transness years before these issues would find their way into the mainstream.

But as advocates and activists know, when it comes to changing people's stances on queerness, there's no substitute for IRL interaction. When James came into the newsroom to write, to edit, to chat, he became the first trans person I'd ever (knowingly) talked to, and his mere presence disarmed any myths I might otherwise have internalized. He was smart, funny, kind. He reminded me of myself in some ways, though it was too early for me to realize just what that meant. We didn't have a ton in common in terms of cultural leanings, but I felt so much more comfortable around him than I did most guys. His was a masculinity that felt decidedly non-toxic, and from then on, trans rights were no longer, as they continue to be for far too many people, a hypothetical to be debated over drinks or in comments sections.

As time passed, I found myself feeling more and more strongly about the subject. I donated to trans people in need and organizations; I retweeted to raise awareness and to convince. When co-workers stumbled through conversations on the subject, my pulse quickened and my breathing shallowed, like it was me they were laughing at. I found myself leaving the office to walk the halls instead. I thought of myself as a good ally—I'd always been an outsider, an awkward fit for the conventional masculinity my last name implied, and I knew I wasn't exactly straight. It wasn't especially surprising that I seemed to care so much about trans issues. Wasn't I, after all, the guy who'd cried at moments of gay tragedy in both *Milk* and *Doubt*, when I never cried at movies?

/

I thought it was a date at first. (The 2010s were, if nothing else, a decade of uncertainty on whether things were dates or not.) I was a month removed from a tough breakup and genuinely flattered. I hadn't felt a particular attraction to Jessie on a physical level, but she was so smart and talented that I wasn't 100 percent sure it mattered. In any case, I would go, and we would see what it was like.

What it was like was a very nice hour or two, followed by a sitcom-level gag reveal when she told me it was time to go, because next she was getting drinks with a thirtysomething guy we both knew. The humiliation! Of having thought I was special enough to be seen as a *date* date when I wasn't; of getting, for lack of a better word, cucked by a balding older man; mostly, of that feeling I had so often—how naive and narrow my understanding of everything always was, my guesses about other people's feelings and intentions so often laughably off the mark.

Still, I must have acquitted myself acceptably, because in the weeks and months that followed, we stayed friends. We went to things together, got coffee, traded Facebook messages, texts, emails. She was the first friend I made—and ultimately, the only friend I made—during my time in the creative writing program whose writing, whose mind, electrified me. As our friendship grew she let me into the walled garden of her life. She told me stories about her father, her half-siblings, her grandparents. She told me about her loves, her fears, her traumas, the genre-resistant novel she was working on, the times she'd gotten way too high as a teen, the famous comedian's podcast on which she was a semi-regular guest. I felt incomparably lucky. And, as I discovered, unlike so many of my friendships, there was never a current of sexual tension bubbling under the surface, that staple of queer social life. She was just great, and I loved her for it—the closest and smartest and kindest and most talented and successful writer friend I had.

Despite the niceness of the friendship, though, or perhaps because of it, I always had a tiny amount of insecurity about it, always felt like she might one day realize she could do better than me. I heard the way some other friends of mine reacted when I said I was friends with Jessie—with jealousy. How had I pulled that off? When she, like so many of my peers after graduation, turned tail and moved to Toronto, we kept on making each other laugh across the six-hour distance, made sure to schedule hangouts with each other each time one of us visited the other's city. We were still friends. Why wouldn't we be?

But then we weren't.

Long before she sent me a friend-breakup email in 2018, something changed. I can't pinpoint when it was, exactly—whether it was one switch being flipped or a series of slow, inescapable changes, like a ship passing through locks—or where it came from, if anywhere. All I knew is that at some point I was grasping at the straws of our friendship, and every exchange we had felt thinner than they used to be and further in time since the last one, and that, already, years before she ended things, I'd started having anxious dreams about her that made me realize how sad I was about what had happened to the friendship, how scared I was of losing it, of losing her. What had I done? She was not the kind of person to be confrontational or to call me on something. I was not the kind of person to ask her what was wrong, afraid of worsening whatever problem I had caused. Our interactions still had the outward tenor of the old ones, they just were lacking somehow, simulacra of friendly exchanges rather than the real thing. At the time, as someone who'd grown up always feeling othered and ostracized, my friendships felt like all I had, and the idea that they could dissipate, could melt into thin air, was too horrifying to consider. Who would I be without her good opinion of me to prop me up?

/

An ironic part—or perhaps a fitting one—of the role Jessie's ending of our friendship played in my coming out is that she had played a role, too, in the very first stirrings of gender identity understanding I had as an adult, long after whatever childhood playfulness had been beaten out of me by the slings and arrows of outrageous cisnormativity: She was the first person to make me feel genuine gender euphoria—that beautiful trans feeling that inverts gender dysphoria, when you feel thrillingly in sync with how you're being perceived.

It was a text message—the first time someone called me "girl" and it wasn't an insult. Women had joined their male counterparts in calling into question my manliness all through my youth, but when Jessie asked me a question—something like "girl, where you at?" in 2011, when I was late to a social event, I perceived in it a beautiful sense of freedom, a full-hearted acceptance of me and my potential to be who and what I wanted to be.

At the time, I rationalized away the specifically gendered aspect of being called "girl" when describing the moment (I *had* to talk about it, so potent was the rush). It was, I wrote to my friend Georgia, like being called "the same, not other." The dream of being accepted by women as one of their own, not a threat, outsider, interloper, was certainly part of the package.

But it wasn't until years afterward that I would be able to acknowledge to myself that *being* a girl (even a laughably little bit, like wearing a bobby pin to keep my unkempt bangs out of my face, or ordering a T-shirt with a feminine design from Etsy and wearing it like it was any other piece of clothing) was what I was aching for, too, the desire so secret, buried so deep that to even articulate it to oneself, like whispering a prayer into your pillow, in the privacy of your locked, completely unlit home, long after all your neighbours have gone to sleep, can still feel risky.

/

The specific instance of hurt Jessie had mentioned in her friend-breakup email was: I had slept with Madeleine, a young Indigenous trans poet Jessie and I had both met in Banff six months earlier, and it had gone badly.

I had felt flattered by the undisguised attraction and attention Madeleine had paid me during the two weeks of the writers' retreat, despite the fact that I'd been in a monogamous relationship at the time. When I found myself single again at the beginning of that summer, we had started sexting with each other, and made plans to meet up in Toronto, where she was staying for a week in a vacationing friend's empty apartment. When she invited me to stay with her so we could hook up, I jumped at the chance, in the slutty haze of my new-found singlehood seeing it as an opportunity to potentially shoot my shot with other crushes in the city as well. The fact that Madeleine was in a pre-existing monogamous relationship, had pushed her boyfriend to agree to let her sleep with me, didn't resonate as it maybe should have. Whereas she saw me as someone worth rewriting the rules of her relationship for, I saw her simply as already taken and so unlikely to care much about having my undivided attention. We were both horny people, that was all.

Things fell apart, predictably. After a first day spent together, I told her I was going on a date with someone else that second night. She responded with surprise and hurt. I felt confused. Why did she care? She had a boyfriend back home in Halifax. On instinct, I told her I wouldn't sleep with this other girl—I wasn't even sure that she liked me, anyway, nor 100 percent confident that it *was* a date at all. Then I left for the evening, first for drinks with a different woman, a long-time crush who kissed me for the first time on a hillside overlooking a baseball diamond, then speed-walked to my actual date, drinks at a rustic little pub called the Gem with B.; B. who I wasn't sure even liked me yet, B. who in a few months would become my official girlfriend and then, many years later, the longest-lasting romantic partner of my life, who today has been my partner for nearly as long as all my other past relationships put together.

My next conversation with Madeleine happened over text, around midnight, me naked in B.'s bed. "You slept with her, didn't you," she asked, accusing. I couldn't lie. "I'm sorry," I said. "I got drunk and forgot completely." It had been a promise made in haste, half-meant, more out of a desire for her not to be mad at me than anything. A liar's promise, an addict's promise. I hadn't thought about what I'd said to Madeleine when B. invited me back to her place, not when she sat on my lap on her living-room couch, not when we stumbled together to her bedroom. Not until I checked my phone. Overdrunk and distractible. "Don't come back here tonight," Madeleine texted. "You can pick up your stuff in the morning." She was twenty-two. I was twenty-nine. Before the past few weeks, I had never really casually hooked up with anyone before. Already I'd made a huge mess of things, had broken something nice, something that couldn't be fixed.

/

After Madeleine kicked me out, the next night's planned get-together with two other members of our Banff cohort, Jessie and another poet we'd gone to school with, was summarily cancelled. I texted Jessie my apologies for having ruined things, to no response. A few weeks later, she emailed me to tell me the friendship was over. The way I'd hurt Madeleine was the last straw for her, but she spent only a single sentence on it. The rest of the email was dedicated to her assessment of me as a kind of male feminist creep. She noted that "multiple women" had told her I'd made them "uncomfortable," that she, too, had felt uncomfortable in conversations with me, that I had a tendency of bringing up sex in conversations with female friends. As I read over the email I felt the sense that a pit had opened up underneath me, that I was being swallowed whole by the earth. In that moment, I wanted nothing so much as to die.

Though, as she had requested, I did not reply, I read and reread Jessie's email over the coming months, parsing it for clues, trying to suss out what she'd meant, what she'd been referring to in her intentionally vague phrasings. Multiple women, uncomfortable. Multiple women, uncomfortable. Multiple women, uncomfortable. What had I done? I racked my brain. Because of my social anxiety, I was almost always at home, barely ever stayed out late, didn't go to half as many literary events as I felt I should. I'd been in a comfortable, boring monogamous relationship for most of the past four years. I was so stringent about my IRL behaviours toward women that I had written an opinion piece on men's duty to go out of their way not to make women feel scared and threatened in public for the student paper back in 2011, long before these were mainstream conversations. Jessie and I had lived in different cities for years now. Who was talking to her about me? What behaviours of mine had caused multiple women to feel uncomfortable? Did I have some kind of shadow self who was acting horribly without my knowledge? I felt like a crazy person.

Ultimately, I settled on the most likely answer: It was my online behaviours. As Jessie had slowly withdrawn ever more from our friendship over the past few years, in my quiet desperation, I had found myself wanting to be friends with her friends, too, to be part of the bubble of cool women in Toronto she surrounded herself with, who all seemed talented, creative, interesting, fun. Hoping that somehow an acceptance from her friend group would confirm the continued survival of our own friendship, that it wasn't really slipping through my fingers for reasons I couldn't then guess at, that I'd only been imagining things. I wanted so badly to be accepted by this group of women who seemed to live the lives I wanted for myself, who had burgeoning creative careers, big follower counts on social media, an aura of something elusive and unattainable, a Toronto glow inaccessible to me in Montreal, far from the centre of Canada's publishing industry. I had followed these women in the hope that they would see in me what I thought Jessie had seen in me originally, that I was smart and funny and Not Like Other Men. Please let me into the … I am normal and can be trusted with …

I hadn't—I wouldn't have—done anything egregious. Over the course of the three or four years Jessie had been in Toronto, I had liked a few too many posts, hearted a few too many stories, made a few too many jokey responses, on main and in the DMs. Not an insane amount—but enough that they had noticed, I supposed. I had been excited by their online presences, had wanted to be playful, had hoped they would see me, that in seeing me, they would confirm that I wasn't Bad, Bad the way being a Man always made me feel. But they weren't there to affirm anything about me—they were living their lives. They didn't see *me*, they saw a Man who was Acting Strangely. Pestering. Trying to Ingratiate. Who wouldn't take the subtle hint of their non-responses, their muted responses, the tones they were trying to hit, the way women are forever straddling the line between polite and disinterested, searching for the exact note that will cause Men to leave them alone without feeling the urge to Get Angry about it.

/

Why did it take me until I was in my thirties to come out? Partly, it was for a lack of models. "Representation matters" feels like the type of over-earnest woke catchphrase that was only ever destined to become a Twitter joke, but as much as representation alone is only one arrow in the quiver of total liberation, it *does* matter. To come out in the fall of 2019 at thirty-one—ancient, in queer terms—and still do so before seeing a single explicitly non-binary character in film or TV? Or before a single celebrity had relinquished their cis male card for the pastures of non-binariness? That's weird! In the six years since, celebs like Sam Smith and Jonathan Van Ness and Cole Escola have made headlines for rejecting binary gender—and Suzy Eddie Izzard's decades-long gender-bending resolved beautifully from a personal eccentricity into a legible queerness—but for a concept that's recognizable enough for an American politician to use they/them pronouns as a cruel joke in his successful 2024 presidential campaign, it still feels so far at the margins of normative culture as to be invisible to most people.

Things weren't much more promising in my own life. While the first non-binary person I ever met was assigned male at birth, or AMAB in the parlance of queer people, for a long time, non-binariness seemed to be much more popular with AFAB members of my social circle. In fact, at times in the early 2020s, it felt like some people saw "non-binary" primarily as an identity for AFAB people who felt out of step with femininity—there was briefly a Twitter hubbub over a short-lived essay that suggested "non-binary" was just a new, woke way of saying "I'm not like other girls"—or a transitional space for people on their way to coming out as "full trans": a few people, after I came out to them, asked me, in coded or not-so-coded ways, whether this might just be a step on my journey, rather than a valid identity for people assigned male at birth.

Ironically, because they had been living life as girls and I as a boy, it was all too easy to recognize my AFAB non-binary pals as genuinely non-binary, to grant them an escape from cisness that I continued to deny myself, though their wish was to move away from exactly what I wanted to move toward—and it felt like, on some level, I was giving them credit specifically because I perceived their closeness to something they did not want for themselves. But for me, from deep within the bear trap of compulsory cisness, non-binariness felt like a Get Out of Jail Free card—something whose liberatory possibilities I coveted, but that I, a disgusting Man, had neither earned nor deserved. But how does a person earn the courage to undo that kind of fate? How big of an eraser do you need to remove the writing on the wall?

/

What Jessie and her female friends didn't know—what I hadn't yet admitted to myself, let alone others—was that I wasn't a man, wasn't Like That. That I was a neurodivergent non-binary person who wasn't always spectacular at social interactions, that they could have said a clear No to me in a thousand different impolite or even cruel ways and I would have apologized for their trouble. This was one of the hardest things to stomach about Jessie's email and the way it elided any real details and closed off any possibility of discussion—the idea that she thought I would react with anger and self-righteousness, rather than with sadness and a desire to apologize, if she told me the truth about what had happened, who had spoken to her about me, the times I had made her feel strange. That I would react, in short, in a Masculine way, rather than in a Feminine way. Maybe she hadn't ever really known me, hadn't ever really seen me, then.

And it hurt—for many years—but it was my fault, I suppose, if it was anyone's, for not yet having been able to clearly articulate what I was and wasn't like. One of the beautiful things about being capital-*Q* Queer is its amorphousness, the way it can allow for the self to shift and transmute and metamorphose, as selves so often do. But on the ground, terminology still matters for so many. Because the context for our actions matters, the same sentences hit different coming out of different people's mouths, and someone who seems like a man trying to blunt-force their way into women's spaces is much more likely to be a predator than a closeted queer person seeking community with the people who most feel like home.

"If you hear hoofbeats, think horses, not zebras" is advice they give to doctors when it comes to matching symptoms to diagnoses. But as so many people who've had their problems misidentified by the medical establishment know, that's not much consolation for those who actually are zebras.

So it was in that context, seeing someone she thought of as an avowed male feminist who didn't understand women's boundaries online and who would casually sleep with a young Indigenous trans woman only to discard her the next night for a white cis woman, that Jessie drew a line in the sand. She was just the first; in the months to come, two other Toronto writer friends also ended their friendships with me after conversations with Madeleine, after Jessie's concerns came to light. Though they deemed me Bad enough to clearly and unambiguously move away from, there were no public posts, no attempts at cancellation, and, as far as I could tell from chance interactions with mutual friends, no whisper network campaign. This cloaked quality made the pain a double-edged dagger—I was spared the crucible of public hatred, but there was also no forum for me to plead my case, and without specifics from Jessie, all I knew for sure that I had done wrong was drunkenly cheating on someone I was not in a relationship with. Though I drafted dozens of apologies in my head and on my laptop, without anything explicitly Wrong to apologize for,

I was too scared to post about it in clear terms, lest I invite responses either positive or negative that I didn't deserve. But without anything out there, there was no way to atone—only a continued stewing in the shame of my feelings of rejection and exile, a pressing on the wound.

My thoughts returned to the scene of the hurt over and over. No matter which way I rotated the situation in my head, one thing felt clear: The way I'd been treated smacked of gender. The friendship breakups felt inextricably linked to the perception of me as a Man. I just couldn't imagine a woman receiving these messages after a summer of being messy, flirty, and thirsty. It wasn't the recognition that I'd been acting strangely, that nearing the end of a difficult relationship, I'd been straddling the line between flirtatious and chill in my interactions with women online, that I'd been a blur of slutty energy that summer, that I'd been callous with other people's feelings, or that I'd felt too ashamed when Jessie had sent her email to tell all but a handful of my closest friends.

It was the reality that, as far as I could tell, those actions only added up to genuinely monstrous if you perceived the person behind them as cis, het, and male—not as person but as predator, as privileged interloper within queer creative communities. In their eyes, maybe I was like nothing so much as a sociopath who'd learned the language of therapy and restorative justice, the better to inflict misery on his victims, just a wolf with an especially convincing sheep costume in its closet.

I imagined what the female version of me that year was like. What her version of the story was. She was going through a hard time. Her girlfriend had never fucked her right, not once, not since the beginning, almost four years ago, but she loved her girlfriend, their story, and everything they had in common, how at home she felt with her, so she tried to pretend that it didn't matter and she knew after a time that trauma was part of the reason, and she didn't want to be the kind of person who ended things with a survivor over sex and nothing else, because what kind of a shallow slut did that make her, so she sat with it, she sat in the tension of her growing desire, stretching like a rubber band, so yes, she found herself developing crushes on friends of hers, yes, she found herself imagining what it would be like if they wanted her back as she was drifting off to sleep and yes, they did all happen to be younger femme-presenting writers, but no, she never made anything that could be even misconstrued as a pass, not even when granted opportunities, she knew what boundaries were, she was great at self-control, and then finally through the fog of sadness and nothing feeling right she started taking the meds, and the meds helped her be less afraid of seeing the truth of the thing that she had to do, which was end the relationship, which had not been happy in so long, though they had tried sex therapy together and it had improved things but it had also made her realize that the gap was unbridgeable, and she did it, she ended things, and then at some point in the month afterward she realized that she'd gone out socializing or drinking every night for three weeks straight, which she'd never done before in her life, not even close, what kind of person was she now, and was this the breakup rebounding like a spring or the therapeutic substance she took a teaspoon of every morning. Or was it both. *I couldn't distinguish the symptoms from my heart.*

That's the woman I felt like. Not the woman I was seen as, though. I imagined that woman being surrounded by support. I imagined her telling her friends she was getting laid with abandon and receiving clapping emojis and requests for detail. I imagined her receiving the benefit of the doubt when things went bad with a hookup. I could not get over how differently our stories had played out.

/

I wasn't short on evidence that something was up, even long before I turned thirty. There was only one man I considered a close friend, but whenever women included me in things I felt thrilled, and whenever trans or genderqueer people seemed to see me as safe, I felt at home. I had only dressed up for Halloween twice since I'd hit puberty, and both times I was an almost comically genderless object. I didn't want to get rid of my penis, though I'd often posed in the mirror naked, tucking it back between my legs. I liked the idea of being called "daddy" in bed, despite in high school harbouring secret fantasies of someday being the world's first pregnant man.

I even had twin tweet drafts on my phone for a long time: "proof i'm a boy" (like sports, look good in jackets) and "proof i'm a girl" (hate men, listened to "hello" by adele 100 times) before an impulse deletion of the app doomed them both to the ether. The childhood photos, the adult misandry that had led me to write my horrible opinion piece, the way I always sided with women, always thought they were right, and good, and special and that men were trash. A slightly self-savvier person might have figured it out. But part of the problem is that being socialized male is sort of like growing up drinking Don't Explore Your Inner Self Too Much juice, and my specific case—endless discomfort and worrying and angst but comparatively little by way of outward evidence, no pull to wear dresses, no secret makeup case at home—made it so tricky to ferret out. There's a different toughness there from the one trans women face.

But knowing where "soft, awkward man" ended and "AMAB non-binary person whose gender dysphoria is more psychological than physical" began was something I wrestled with for years before taking the plunge, and I'm genuinely not sure how long it would have taken me to get there had not the hurt of those friend breakups forced me to spend that time thinking seriously about who I was and how I was read. For a year and a half or so after those fateful few months in 2018, I spent every waking moment on some degree of alert as to whether the next interaction I had with a peer or friend would be another accusation, another ostracization. My rejection sensitivity dysphoria in overdrive.

But as much as Jessie's denial of me had hurt, I owed her one. In that moment she had started the countdown clock on my coming out. She had made my gender identity something I could no longer sweep under the rug of myself.

In the summer of 2019, an online acquaintance who was an editor at a lit mag I had sent a poem to asked me, unprompted, about my pronouns. "I left them out of my bio intentionally," I said, "because I'm not really sure about them right now." "Oh," she said. "I wasn't asking because of your bio—just curious about you." I laughed. "I think my pronouns are ______/______ right now," I said.

/

In order to win an argument, often the best approach is to reject your opponent's terms entirely. When the other side is challenging whether a certain type of person genuinely deserves mercy, to say not that the person does because of X, Y, and Z, but that the person does because there is no point at which a person stops deserving compassion, to throw out the logics of carcerality, violence, and revenge entirely.

Ultimately, that was how I came to be comfortable with my own non-binariness. It was easier to take the facts on the ground—the fact that gender had, to quote the Wachowski sisters, always felt like a splinter I couldn't get out—than to legislate what exactly it meant for me to be just Girl enough to no longer be Boy, how feminine I had to be exactly to be a real non-binary person. Like being in love or being a cop, being a man is something you have to want, and it had been years and years of restless wrestling since I had.

In my late teens, I had engaged in another, similar process with the god I used to believe in. It had started with feelings of doubt, grew to include research and thought exercises, and ended with a final, irreversible switch being flipped. Here, too, it began with that discomfort, before graduating to the next level. At one point I interviewed two AMAB non-binary people for an article about How to Know If You're Non-Binary. The piece was never published, but I recognize in retrospect what I'd been doing. Why I'd been curious about a question like that in the first place. Not long afterward, I stopped gendering myself as male in conversation. Just to see what it would be like.

/

My first years as an out non-binary person were a process of navigation, finding my way through the giant corn maze of gender. Memes on Twitter taught me that it's normal and expected for lesbians to stay in touch with each other years after a single date, but the proliferation of male exes reaching out to women from their past "innocently" in the early months of the COVID pandemic was evidence of malfeasance and masculine toxicity. When I wanted to be in touch with someone from my past, which of these two was I, I wondered? Toxic or adorable? Or a bit of both? Where, exactly, was the tipping point?

I had come out, I was living a life where people they-ed me, I began incorporating feminine modes of presentation into my look, bought clip-on earrings, painted my nails, or, more often, got my partner to paint them for me, wore bobby pins more often, dyed my hair—pink mostly, though it clashed with my complexion. I felt closer to my true self than I ever had before, and yet.

At some point I recalled a non-binary person I saw retweeted onto my feed occasionally, bedecked in makeup and, from my perspective, thriving. Let's call them Robin. I had known Robin first by reputation, years prior, as a cis man who was "creepy," who had gone on dates with a few female friends of mine only to profess undying love within days or even hours. In retrospect, it seemed obvious that, like me, in their interactions with women, Robin was working through a complicated relationship to femininity—one for which there was not yet a clear personal or cultural script for either participant.

To be creeped out is to perceive a threat that has not been made legible, to substitute perception for reality as a means of getting ahead of a potential danger. I don't blame these women for being creeped out by me or Robin or anyone acting out the secret or unspoken desires of the self—but it strikes me that a core component of creepiness is acting in ways that are abnormal.

Not threatening, not malicious—just ... abnormal. And trans people know all too well to what degree quote-unquote *normal* is both out of reach and, ultimately, not worth pursuing.

/

One of the saddest outcomes of Jessie's email was that, in the years that followed, it made it nearly impossible for me to trust completely in the friendships of others, to believe that they would like me in a lasting way, to have faith that they would catch me if I fell, to understand that sometimes people grow apart and that's okay. Particularly during a global pandemic of historical proportions that severely impacted my comfort levels with the mainstays of socializing for half a decade thereafter.

For a long time after Jessie's email, it felt like every friendship became at least a little bit fraught, every period of radio silence turned into an ominous, wordless warning: *You are bad and I am pulling back.* I let things slip and slide away with various female friends like that, telling myself if they wanted me in their lives they would reach out. One such friend went from one of the more consistent presences in my life in my twenties to almost out of it entirely in my thirties. We ran into each other once at the Olympic Stadium in 2021, each of us coincidentally getting our second dose of the COVID vaccine, and we walked and talked and took a selfie together. And then barely spoke again for the next four years.

When I finally drummed up the courage to ask her what had happened, she admitted there had been no great inciting incident. We had just never been that close, in her opinion, had started talking less and less, and she had moved on. When she did a major cull of her Instagram followers a while back, I just hadn't made the cut. I sat with that. How little I meant, in the grand scheme of things. How Jessie's blunt ending had reinvested my self-image with the idea that other people were talking behind my back, were thinking about my actions, were judging me harshly. But they weren't. I wasn't the star, wasn't the centre of attention, was just me. I was a person—that thing I'd spent so much time wanting to be, during those years when I felt so keenly the unpleasantness of being gendered wrong.

/

At some point, anyway, I realized something about Jessie's breakup email, the way she'd communicated, through the haze of her vagueness, that she couldn't have me going around using her name. I realized I was walking in the paths of my queer forebears when I'd told people I was a friend of Jessie's in the hope of showing them that I wasn't like other guys: I remembered that gay men used to say they were friends of Dorothy's.

For them, using the phrase in place of articulating a truth about their desires was about safety. For me, it was a path of least resistance. It's so much simpler to bury a secret about how you deviate from the idea of *man* in a woman's name. My mistake was in imagining that Jessie's good opinion of me meant more than my own truth about who I really was, in believing it was easier to outsource my PR to a beacon of feminism than to imagine I might be most believable as myself.

It is a blog post I wrote in November 2008 where I grappled with feelings about gender, where I wrote down these sentences after reading that article in *The Atlantic* about trans kids: "Obviously, my problem is not even remotely on the level of a seven-year-old boy saying, 'Look, Mommy, I'm a girl!' with his penis tucked between his legs. But there's an issue, obviously." An email I wrote in September 2010 but never sent, where I grappled with feelings about gender, where I wrote down these sentences: "I don't know how much I actually want to be a woman—I don't think it's a transsexuality thing—but I do know that I don't want to be a *man* in the way men are, and are thought of, today." It is wishing I had known back then that there were other options. It is how the gender binary is a net that is thrown over us over and over and over and over and over. A net from which some people wish to disentangle themselves. A net for whose ropes I am seeking out a sword. A knife. Something to cut with.

Ligatures

"Simp" is a psyop, Dostoevsky maintained that you have a moral imperative to yearn for a woman
—@Galaxriel, Twitter

an ugly man serial liking your instagram stories feels like being chased in the woods
—@killmeorshutup, Twitter

THERE'S A COSMOLOGICAL PHENOMENON known as tidal locking that works like this: one object orbiting another rotates as it orbits so that one side of a planet or moon is always facing in, and one is always facing out. We experience this on Earth; that's where the phrase "the dark side of the moon" comes from. Though which side is lit and which side is in shadow changes as the moon rotates relative to the sun, one side of it is always hidden to us on Earth, and one side is always facing us.

My first English professor in college—in the Quebec-only CEGEP system, two years between high school and university—taught me that light was a metaphor for knowledge. That which is illuminated is known, and that which is dark is unknown. Within this framework, whichever side of the moon we cannot see is always in this darkness of unknowability. So, dark. Even if not.

This professor was later the subject of a scandal, for sleeping with a student, a young man who'd come to him to ask what to do about an affair he had already been having with another professor. Desire makes us do strange things. *And God said, Let there be light.*

However, if two objects that are tidally locked to one another are close enough in size—rather than a clear planet/moon situation where one dwarfs the other, for instance—it is known as a binary system. Two celestial bodies spinning around each other, forever entwined in a cosmic folie à deux.

I think about things like this sometimes when I think about attraction. Of course in English we use the same word to denote both physical laws and romantic or sexual feelings. *The Laws of Attraction*. The scene in *Oppenheimer* when he touches a woman he will go on to sleep with, explaining quantum physics. How the atoms stop his hand from passing through hers.

But the truth of the matter is that, for all the strength of the pull keeping them together, the pull keeping these two bodies apart is equally powerful. What is it like, to be held in stasis by your relationship to a thing, always close but never touching, a cross-section of two parallel lines?

So often, I am a tidally locked body, orbiting something I am inexorably both drawn toward and held at bay from. Which is to say, for as long as I can remember, the only thing I've really cared about is crushes.

/

Simone Weil said attention, taken to its highest degree, is a form of prayer. As it turns out, for those who feel starved of it, even a middling degree of attention can feel distinctly holy.

As a bad bisexual, my attractions to men and masc-of-centre people have always been a little humdrum—few and far between; there, and real, but nothing to write home about. But there have been years of my life when it felt like the most memorable thing that happened to me was this girl or that girl paying attention to me in some way that felt different, and that's all I could think about for days or weeks or months afterward. A little tuning fork, vibrating with the sheer intensity of how it felt to have been noticed.

I say girl, I suppose, and not woman because I recognize that the sentiment was one I carried with me from long before I was an adult. After a time, the girls in these memories did grow up and become women, and not infrequently they came out as non-binary people, too, but how feminine they were exactly never felt like the point—it was just an awareness of someone more feminine than me, of their having something beautiful and true that I could never really touch, of hoping however briefly to be cast in their spotlights. Of hoping they would see something good and true in me, too.

Through the years, these fleeting flutters of attention that peppered my life would leave me gasping in their wake, messaging people for second opinions, doodling my little poems in my little laptop, tracing and retracing the outline of the moment in my memory like a zealot. I can remember with crystal-clear clarity moments from decades past when one of these crushes paid attention to me like that. Not romantic, maybe even not intentional, but just—different. Enough to elevate it from ground into figure. The way moments of pure pleasure shrink the universe down to a peach pit, and tomorrow might not come, for the sheer force of your caring.

If we are the things we care about, who am I if not a collection of the memories I have of the crushes I used to have?

I am 's eyebrows arching in the doorway, arms crossed. letting me speak first in biology class. *She noticed!* sitting down right in front of me when I was on the couch, letting her back rest against my shins. Impromptu hand-holding walking with through the Plateau. The way hugged me when I left the New Year's party early. - stroking my arm as she walked by, a few New Years later. 's brush on my shoulder at the basement reading. The way invited me up after I walked them home, offering to let me come to bed. saying "I can't believe you're single," archly, online, in response to a dumb tweet. *She noticed!* The long, long goodbye hug and I held and the way we each texted each other about it at the same moment fifteen minutes later. I am the way liked a run of my IG pictures around 3 or 4 a.m. one night, seemingly unafraid of what that might say. I am seeming to sneak a photo of me from across the table the night we met. I am playing with their hair in my apartment after poetry group. , at that one wedding, slapping my knee after a joke, like they do in the movies, a year after I'd written a poem about my feelings for her. I am 's excited, youthful DMs, stripping down naked to go swimming with me in the quarry, assuming I would know that quarry swimming meant skinny-dipping. The way said, "Oh, you'd *love* Vancouver" the first night we met, as if she already knew me, years before she was famous. Then, , actually in Vancouver, later still, offering to let me crash at her place: "But I don't have a couch, though." The implication being.

What to do with all the people in my life I feel this longing for? Often I think about how, more than anything, I just want to be able to admit it. Maybe this is my Christian self feeling the weight of a lie. *You have heard that it was said, "You shall not commit adultery"; but I tell you that everyone who gazes at a woman to lust after her has committed adultery with her already in his heart.*

I don't want anything from a crush so much as to just not feel obligated to hide it away like a shameful secret. I want to sit down with each one and say, "I find you beautiful, do you find me anything?" And just talk about that over tea or something. And then hug goodbye and go back to the way things were. I want to be trapped overnight in a slumber party situation, perhaps by extreme snowfall, at the age of twelve, with the people I was in love with when I was twelve, and open up to them about myself, and see whether we would connect.

My first date with someone I'd go on to be in a relationship with: February 15th, 2013. After we had kissed, finally, in their bed, me breathlessly telling them, "I thought you were so beautiful the first moment I saw you, I've been thinking about this ever since then." Later they told me how cringe that was. I'd thought it was romantic. But it was just a dam bursting. Now feeling like I had permission to set down the secret. My skinny Atlas arms trembling from the weight.

What a useless want. But what to do with all these feelings? How to hold them without burning my fingers, how to let them go without singeing the other? How to express them here, without fearing that I sound crazy—crazy to some for having too much desire, crazy to others for obsessing over the perfectly normal human experience of crushing a lot. What was wrong with me? I wondered. What a slut I am.

/

Of course, at some point I noticed a thread running through many of those examples.

So many of them were instances of girls I had a pre-existing interest in—whether that interest spanned fifteen minutes or fifteen years—touching me without first asking for permission. This is part of the crazy of crushes, the calculations you're endlessly running through in your head. She loves me, she loves me not. *Un peu, beaucoup, passionnément, à la folie, pas du tout.* Of course people touch other people all the time, it's only normal, it's part of life, we live in a society, only a sad person raised in a sick culture would think little moments like these meant something special.

But of course they all meant something; women don't just go around intentionally touching male-presenting people wantonly, willy-nilly. Each touch a confirmation that I had been right. That there was *something* between us. But how many of them meant what I thought they meant? Wordless touch can signify so many things. Infinite gradations of intimacy. I see you. I trust you. You're funny. Maybe, in another lifetime. You're like a brother to me. Thank God.

These thoughts eventually rolled over into others. I started thinking about all the instances of women discussing grappling with the feelings of attraction they sometimes felt for men who had crossed their boundaries, whether violently or subtly. I remember, when I first encountered such admissions, thinking about how sad they were, an admission that these women had been broken in some way by the men who'd violated them, that it was possible to leave a lasting mark on someone via cruelty that not only scarred them but also warped them in some way. That made them want what was bad for them. That left them orbiting around a moment of impact. A small hurt with incredible mass. The density of sexual boundaries being broken.

I see, now, having recognized these same tendencies in myself, how sad and small that reading was. How wrong I'd been. I thought about them now through the lens of my own experiences. I wondered if instead what was happening was: If you spend your whole life wanting to be touched, even a touch that breaks certain rules can feel more affirming than no touch. I wondered if what was happening was: Bad things sometimes occur to people who are already so attuned to wanting sexual attention that certain forms of cruelty or inappropriateness coming from certain specific people can feel preferable to being ignored completely.

/

In 2013, I was a part—in some sense or other—of a fledgling literary movement. It was called "alt lit," and for a handful of years, it collected together weirdos on the internet into a loose digital community (nominally worldwide, but largely based in the US) focused on writing to, in, around, and about the online world.

Alt lit seemingly sprang from nowhere, but was bolstered by emerging and mainstream internet technologies—Facebook, Twitter, GChat and Gmail played outsized roles not just in how the community was built, but also in the writing it produced; characters in short stories would email each other back and forth, poems at times felt like lists of tweets (and in some cases, were). IRL readings were broadcast using since-shuttered live-streaming apps like Justin.tv, people developed noms de plume or even wholesale internet personas, and it became normal to add dozens or hundreds of strangers on Facebook in a spammy form of literary networking.

What was exciting to me and many other people drawn to the alt lit concept was the sense that everything was rewritable—the rules of socializing, of publishing, of fiction, of poetry, even of spelling and grammar. Perhaps more than anything else, alt lit felt like a space of possibility.

But, on the other hand, perhaps more than anything else, it was also a space of sexual inappropriateness. The whole thing came to a grinding halt a few years later following multiple accusations of rape toward the founder of one of alt lit's most well-known online magazines. Not long afterward, a friend of his—and possibly alt lit's most visible member—a poet slash vlogger, faced accusations of grooming and sexualized messaging with minors. A third, less successful alt lit writer admitted, unprompted, to raping someone. Some of the movement's leading female figures, like Frank Hinton and Lucy K Shaw, advocated for tearing the movement's online spaces down. It was hard not to feel like the whole thing had been a sham, a hastily erected series of structures that, though they claimed to push back against and do away with the traditional publishing models, seemed to exactly mirror the way literary communities have long been spaces of sexual misconduct where powerful men use their reputations to sleep with young, up-and-coming female writers.

For me, alt lit was also the first place where I was flashed.

/

One of my first sessions with my therapist—perhaps the second one, even—dealt with the fears I had of scaring women out in public. I talked about the wrestling I did with myself when walking by a woman I sensed might be attractive, the trying not to look, despite the always pull to do just that, how wrong and bad that felt, that I knew the gaze could be violent. My therapist said that this was partially testosterone in action. *Some of my trans clients start to feel this way after starting T.* That helped, a little bit. If not an excuse then at least a reason. Again it felt the slightest bit religious. An ineffable thing, a curse, something coming over me, an inverted Holy Spirit. Flames softly licking at the skull.

It was my whirlwind summer. I was expending a lot of energy then, and had been for a long time, and continue to do so to this day, worrying about how women might be scared of me. To wit, a message I sent a guy friend a few months beforehand: "I've asked like 20 women to spend time alone with me in some form since [a.] and i broke up and i don't have a single no yet."

Many of these had been dates in the traditional sense, but many were not—friend hangs, or amorphous interactions containing an amount of attraction but not turning into anything. The phrasing of my message, and my insistence of merging these two categories, feels telling. Between the lines, I was not crowing about conquest—I was proud because I was not considered a threat. *Spend time alone with me.* Not fuck, not kiss, not go on a date—*spend time alone with me.* How pathetic and scared I was of being creepy.

What I wanted was to be desired in some form, as friend, as lover, as crush—as company. But, most of all, to be trusted. Because what hurt most about being perceived as a man was the feeling, deep in my bones, that I would always be threat first and anything else second.

This came back to me years later when reading about the erotic thrill of being a sub. I began to wonder. If submissive people enjoy giving up control in bed in order to re-enact, in a safe context, experiencing violence, do doms enjoy taking control in order to do an inverted version of the same thing? When I got off on the idea of a woman wanting me to hold her down or tie her up, was I also rewriting the scripts, alchemizing the feeling that an aggressor, a violator was all I could be into a narrative where that was what was wanted, that was what was desired? Was it a way to heal from the pain of being feared, of being seen as one who'd hurt? Of course this pain was a far lesser kind than the pain of fearing, the pain of being hurt. But it was not nothing. And it had not gone away.

/

When I came out as non-binary one of my oldest friends struggled with the change. "But you're a guy," she said. "All we ever talk about is the girls you like." But gender identity and sexual orientation have never been the same thing, though they're sometimes easy to transpose and may appear interchangeable to the uninitiated. And, in fairness, the word *queer*, like a cloud passing over the moon, blurs all to smudge. It's just that you're: different.

But any lesbian could tell you that liking girls does not make a person a guy, and any gay man—or, for that matter, any ace or aro man—could tell you that being a guy does not require one to like girls. If anything, I thought, later, the feverishness of my attraction was, in some way, effeminate. Roland Barthes: "It follows that in any man who utters the other's absence something feminine is declared: this man who waits and who suffers from his waiting is miraculously feminized."[34] I cared too much about what my crushes thought, would sacrifice it all for feminine attention. They were my gods. I was not even a priest; I was a simple congregant, prostrating myself in the temple. It was not, or did not feel like, a particularly manly way of being attracted to women.

Did I want to fuck and dominate them in stereotypical ways? I did. Had I asked to want these things? I had not. Did I sometimes wish I was more of a sub or a bottom, for fear of how straightforwardly cishet and masculine my desire felt? I did. Did I actually want to be a sub or a bottom? I did not. And maybe how neatly all this fit into "when a man loves a woman" stock heterosexuality held me back from feeling queer enough to count for a long time. For me and for my friend who wasn't so sure.

How had I come to these desires, anyway? The uncharitable reading is watching porn. But there is porn of lots of things, and I have watched many clips and felt unmoved by what was happening and, not infrequently, saddened, perturbed, disgusted. One of the most gender-affirming truths I have is that I honestly and genuinely find the stories that set up the porn clips hotter than the action itself. The mechanical in-out so often almost meaningless. Yet how many times I'd rewind to rewatch the dialogue at the beginning. The part right when the two decide they will have sex with each other, that is my climactic moment. The infinite sexual power that exists in this little thing, this moment of giving in, a kind of atom of human interaction. How much power could be released from its splitting.

No, I thought. The real reason I had come to find things hot was what had been asked of me, what had been brought up. What had arisen, in bed. A kind of sexual Show and Tell. Exes, flings, hookups. *Slap me in the face. Choke me. Let's do it without a condom. Harder. Cum in me.* Calling me "daddy" without asking. One, though she was older than me. The other, without meaning it to be sexual. But then finding that it was. And getting so wet from it, I was shocked. These things later remaining, unerased, on the page of me. A faint trace. A sexual palimpsest. And then I found myself asking for these things from other people. Wanting to recreate those feelings. It had been someone else's thing and now it was my thing. Passed from one person to the other in the act, almost like an STI. I've read that ideas are like viruses.

/

34 Roland Barthes, *A Lover's Discourse: Fragments*, trans. Richard Howard (Hill and Wang, 2010).

Of course, I'd seen naked bodies without expecting to before, both online and in real life. I'd been around to see guys moon their teammates in the hockey locker room when I was twelve, had stumbled upon porn online, had looked up at the wrong moment in changing rooms. But alt lit was the first context in which someone intentionally showed me, specifically, their naked body without warning or consent, in a situation where it wasn't expected or warranted, in such a way that it made me feel the way flashing makes you feel—weird, and bad, and shy, and ashamed. And later, angry. Bodies are dangerous.

In my case, my alt lit boundary-crosser was also a talented, well-known writer, someone with a real book deal, someone who seemed to be friends with other alt lit luminaries, who'd been written about in places like *Slate*, *Esquire*, and *Vice*. But in my case, it was a woman.

Alice Harrington—like many people in the community, her whole online life took place pseudonymously, but this is a pseudonym of that pseudonym—was, presumably, someone many people wanted to see naked. The cover of her book of short stories is a picture of her face, a demure, beautiful yet bookish woman who might serve as a muse for a tortured artist: black hair with bangs, pale skin, and haunting, searching eyes, at once innocent and knowing. Her stories all seemed to revolve around sex and power, so maybe it shouldn't have surprised me that our conversation boiled down to just that.

She was one of the many people I added on Facebook around that time, and I felt like an unlikely lottery winner when, one night, without warning or prior interaction, she video-called me. I didn't know what to make of it, but I was, as many young writers unexpectedly talking to more successful ones know, excited to feel chosen. She was someone I felt an attraction toward—partly physical, partly intellectual. On some level, she was someone I wanted to be, an idealized version of something, a vision of what it might be like if I could be successful and beautiful all at once.

On the call, she refused to speak aloud; when I spoke, she typed responses in the chat box. We interacted for what must have been an hour, over the course of which she moved around in her apartment, carrying the laptop with her from her bedroom to the kitchen and back. I remember flashes of facts—the feeling of green walls, maybe bordering on turquoise. At some point she got under her covers. At some point later, she got out from under the covers.

What I remember is: She wasn't wearing clothes anymore. What I remember is: She was lying on her right elbow, propped up, splayed out, like a reclining nude in a painting. What I remember is: I was in a relationship.

My brain sort of shut down. I remember stammering—or maybe typing out—that I had to go. I had no idea how to react. I closed the window. A short circuit.

Of course, in my head afterward, I played out all the thoughts one plays out: Had I invited it, somehow? Why had she done that? Was this something she'd done with other people? Was it normal for her, and was I the one who seemed weird? The image of her, electric in my brain. Like, perhaps, she had wanted.

/

I think if straight men were braver, they'd admit they are afraid of being attracted to women. Much has been made of the vagina as a site of fear, a pit into which one might stumble, the maw of desire, a black hole pulling them away from themselves, into the unconsciousness of lust. I think about their names for women who use that propensity to make a living: *She's a hooker. Let's visit the rippers.* The violence of those terms. To rip, to hook. Yes, sex work is work. Because it works on men. Simmering under the surface of the fun and games, there is an extractive quality. Though I have a different relationship to women and femininity, I am not unfamiliar with these mechanics. I cannot count the number of times I have liked a sexy selfie—a thirst trap, after all—and felt like I was paying a tithe, giving an offering to an uncaring god, prone, supplicating.

But the straight men alive today are so bad at articulating desire in a complex way. It feels like there is an enormous, cavernous silence where any kind of discourse about this stuff might be. Faced with the choice between sounding sexist and saying nothing, they have mercifully chosen muteness. But there is then such a poverty to the conversation around desire.

I get it. I myself have put my foot in my mouth trying to navigate these things before. I tried to speak something into that silence once, a few years ago, in a since-deleted tweet: "the reason there are so few lesbians relative to the general population is that almost no one is capable of being attracted to women while having non-zero emotional intelligence. it'll just blow your fuses off."

A friend of mine DMed me to ask what on earth I was trying to say. What I was trying to say was: It hurts so much, being attracted to women all the time. There are so many interesting, beautiful, brilliant, funny, kind, thoughtful, talented, heart-rending women in the world, and sometimes I wished I was less susceptible to feeling attracted to them.

I'd literally joked at times about wanting to castrate myself. Which was partly gender dysphoria, of course, but partly the sense that, without my testes, I might find my sex drive dropping away, might find my thoughts unclouded by the dust of desire, might feel like I imagine certain well-to-do retirees sometimes feel—the rest of their lives stretching out before them, all things possible, no constraints. That's not how it works, of course. But it was nice to imagine.

/

In my late teens and early twenties, my two most emotionally significant exes lived a ten-minute walk from each other, not far from the apartment my mother and sister moved to after my parents' divorce. For a time, coming home after a family dinner, I would find myself choosing to walk rather than take public transit, would find myself coursing through the night streets like water over a plain, slowly creating a riverbed, each path reinforcing the likelihood that next time I'd take the same path, eroding a wet desire line into the ground with just the weight of my footsteps. Here, too, feeling pulled like a magnet. Wending my way past the houses where my exes lived. An unholy pilgrim treading a path to and from temples where I once worshiped. Just to be in proximity for a few seconds, without stopping, to places where I'd felt emotions, once. Just to pass within a block of them, perhaps. Not yet over the addiction.

I sometimes think about this logic—that love is gravity, that attraction is physical pull, that there is something mathematical and unavoidable about it—when I encounter discourse on the subject of men's arousability. The high school memos reminding the girls not to distract the boys with their outfits. How many men cannot help but make crude comments. Like some sort of knee-jerk reaction, the image of a woman walking by appearing on their retinas. A hammer to a specific nerve. How scary that is. That society functions in a kind of tense compromise. That people in power look at young women and think it would be easier to control, cover, cloister, defuse certain bodies than others. Like the way all these mayors of all these cities keep taking money away from services that help people and keep giving them to the cops. Because, I think, they're afraid. Of making them angry.

The universe loves making the same shapes over and over: the circle of both planet and star, the hexagons in beehives and snowflakes, the Fibonacci spirals of shells and hurricanes. So much of attraction for me and for so many was based on looks. A fundamentally meaningless trait. I knew first-hand the way the brain alchemized things into myth. Bone structure, skin tint, a certain cut or style of hair. The shock of seeing someone who looks like an ex. How many times had this happened? Feeling drawn to. A moment of recognition once in a café when a woman about my mother's age walked in with her daughter, the sister of a childhood crush, age six or so, and I watched it telescope out in memory. How (a late-twenties dalliance) had reminded me of (an early-twenties relationship) who'd reminded me of (a teenage crush) who'd reminded me of (a tween-age crush) who'd reminded me of (a childhood crush). Daisy chain of transference *mise en abyme*. What was desire? Rube Goldberg device of the brain. Flip-book blur of faces, traits layered on top of each other. Nothing was special. I was just a sad machine. Neurons firing.

/

I spoke, the next day, to a mutual alt lit friend about what had happened. I needed to tell someone; specifically, I needed to tell someone who knew who the hell Alice Harrington was. I didn't call it a violation, or inappropriate. I just said it was wild.

I got an angry message from Alice a day or two later. Unbeknownst to me, the friend I'd told went and posted a screenshot of the text exchange to her Tumblr, and word had gotten back. I apologized profusely. I wanted her to like me.

Though the cruelty of her move was relatively minor, Alice was, I'd come to realize a decade later, operating from the traditional abuser playbook: cow your victim into silence by making them feel like your bad treatment of them was normal, and their telling people about it was the real violation. But none of that was clear to me at the time. I tried to curry favour with her a year or so later when she put out a public call asking for unpaid copy editing on a piece she was writing for a well-known publication. I offered my services and felt stung when she accepted them but dropped in conversation that she'd gotten the same piece looked at by others.

I was just a face in the crowd then, and I likely had been around when she flashed me. I mentioned it to another writer I knew, someone who'd been peripherally involved in alt lit, and he confessed that she'd impromptu video-chatted him, too, though I can't remember, now, whether she had exposed herself to him. Either way, I wondered whether she did this to all the boys. What was she seeking, exactly?

Though for the most part her writing career went dark after her debut short story collection and the general collapse of alt lit, I'd hear her name brought up from time to time years later. I found myself opening up about the story, hoping that people would take my side, never feeling entirely satisfied with the responses. Of course, I thought, it's different when a woman flashes someone than when a man does. But what she did was still wrong, right? There may not have been any aura of menace to it, and it was digital in nature, the two of us separated by hundreds of miles, but it was non-consensual sexual exposure along unequal power lines within a creative community. It made me feel weird, and bad, and I wished she hadn't done it, though, then as now, I thought she was beautiful, and some part of me still wanted her to like me.

Of course I know how meaningless this all sounds. How frivolous to complain, as someone who's always presented masculine, about seeing a woman's naked body on a screen. Or having my ass slapped by a co-worker once. Or being drunkenly kissed on the cheek once by a gay guy who had a crush on me. Or being sent nudes by a Tinder match as a kind of punishment, to show how angry she was when I said I wouldn't be able to talk as much in the coming days once my partner was back from vacation. Two photos of her topless in the shower. A punctuation mark, a door slammed on the conversation. Not responding to my confused reply. Feeling then how so many women have felt in the past few decades: *You sent that just to make me feel bad.* The shock of it.

I know it sounds like I'm making a mountain of a molehill. It's just something I think about sometimes.

/

Though it's not a direct line, the relationship between our lived experiences, our inner torments, our private struggles, and our desires does not seem to be a tenuous one. In the lead-up to the publication of my last book, I found myself turning with regularity to two sources of erotic material for stress release: ASMR JOI videos and mind-control hentai manga. It seems strange to attempt to write about these things free from shame and unafraid of judgment; of course, all sexual desire is perversion, which means, per a lesson I learned from an animated superhero movie once, that none of it is.

I think I was mostly into the ASMR because I was anxious. What was most fascinating was probing into why I found mind-control hentai manga so arousing. What did I like about seeing black-and-white illustrations of beautiful women losing control of their bodies, their selves? What did I like about seeing them bent to the wills of men? What did I like about watching these feminine bodies become pliable, pleasure seeking, and complacent? Susceptible to orgasm at a moment's notice? Mouldable, like clay?

At some point I realized these stories were the inversion of my own, that what I found erotic in these mind-control narratives was the echo, the reflection of how desire felt to me, how it had always felt like to me—that is to say that it was an external force that came on seemingly without warning, without my consent, turning me into a kind of puppet. In my first book, a poetry collection, poems that compared desire to too-hot peppers making me cough, to bright-green shoots piercing through cloves of garlic like alien chestbursters. That in some sense, when we are aroused, we are zombies, un-selves, acting out wishes not exactly our own. There's a reason people often respond with a kind of disgust to the erotic material they were masturbating to upon completion or other forms of interruption—we are in an instant brought back to our original selves, after having undergone a transformation. Post-nut clarity. We must confront the things that Mr. Hyde has wrought, the dark webpages he has taken it upon himself to visit.

/

Reading Tracy Clark-Flory's *Want Me: A Sex Writer's Journey Into the Heart of Desire,* I encounter again the problem of your politics and kinks not lining up, how horrified Clark-Flory feels as a feminist getting off on decidedly problematic porn. The unpleasantness of this, a conundrum I and so many people have wrestled with throughout history. But it makes me wonder about the gender-flipped version of this particular pickle. I wonder how frequently men find themselves horrified by their desires. It must happen.

Male desire is seen as much scarier than female desire, so I understand that Clark-Flory's problematic fantasies are ones where she or other women are being victimized, for lack of a better word. But what I notice is she does not spend time writing about the question of how to feel when you occupy the other side of the dynamic. After all, it is a dynamic—you cannot meaningfully be dominated without someone to dominate you.

What does participating in the domination do to a person? This question is often elided—understandably, perhaps—by people writing about their experiences of being subjected to the things we think about when we think about rough sex. In Rachel Thompson's *Rough: How Violence Has Found Its*

Way Into the Bedroom and What We Can Do About It, she explores stories of young men enacting these kinds of things on female partners, assuming or believing that this is what most or all women want or expect from a man, moved to violence not out of selfishness and arousal, but out of a grudging sense of duty.

This may not be the most common experience, but it's far from unique. As bell hooks well knows, many people assigned male at birth, whether they come to identify otherwise or not, are inherently gentle souls, and a lifetime of being pushed to act like someone you're not is exhausting and unhealthy, no matter what it is about yourself that you are being denied access to.

Though these things would later go on to take on an erotic context for me, in my twenties, when partners would ask me to enact some form of patriarchal violence on them, I responded with consternation rather than excitement. In 2018, during my whirlwind summer, I found myself being asked to slap a hookup in the face during sex. It wasn't the first time, though the prior request, from half a decade earlier, had been phrased as "Hit me," a request that, in retrospect, was perhaps just "Slap me" verbalized by someone for whom English was not their mother tongue. For me at the time, the semantic gap between hitting and slapping was enough to make the first request feel impossible, to prompt the end of the sexual moment, though I can't remember for sure whether I cried.

The second time around, with a different person, someone I knew less well, asking me to slap her, I was ultimately able to push through my initial concern. Walking together to a social gathering afterward, I told her: "I get it now. Slapping is just the spanking of the face." She responded with scorn, something to the effect of "Stop speaking if you want me to ever fuck you again," although we never did, anyway. Something about the earnestness of my tone—or perhaps just hearing someone trying to make sense of a desire that she did not want to see brought into the realm of the knowable.

When another sexual partner that summer asked to be slapped as well, I was happy to oblige her with a taste of my new-found skill. By mid-August, I found myself suggesting it to yet another hookup, who agreed to it and then, slapped, immediately said, "Actually, no. I don't like being slapped." I was jarred back to reality, felt foolish, uncouth, a tinge of monstrous. She had clearly and immediately communicated consent when I asked, but to have suggested something violent that so immediately revealed itself as unwanted felt terrible.

/

A poem I wrote for the as-yet unpublished collection about religion explored the cheap trick of etymology, the little links that can be found between different words if you study their genealogies for long enough. In the poem, I wound my thoughts together with a braid of other words, trying to muddy the waters of the point I was making, but the original strand contained these lines:

The root of religion   is bondage.

The root comes   from Latin.

religare: to bind

          It's like a ligature,

that little quirk that links   two letters,

bonding them in holy matrimony   in

fluids,   flying things,   flowers,

bound and tossed.

Because as well as being crass and horrible, sex is holy, too, both above and below the experience of being human. To find oneself in desire not just animal, but cog—a participant in a human-making machinery going back not just millennia but thousands of millennia, eons and epochs, until the pieces fitting, running, rutting together become less and less recognizable as human, until they are distinctly not, then not even mammals, then not even fucking. Just cells. Merging. We are just life slowly moving through time.

I think the craziest thing about sex is how porous we are about it. I think often of a specific comic strip, from a webcomic called *Achewood,* a cult-classic online text that follows the lives of a group of anthropomorphic animals living in California. As one of the main characters is agonizing over whether or not to propose to his girlfriend, he's ruminating on the fact that some utterances can't be taken back. The final panel of the strip shows him dressed up in a stereotypical fifties getup, in front of the caption "NATIONAL SENTENCE COUNCIL":

"Built just like regular sentences, these sentences can in an instant transform forever the life of their speaker!"[35]

This is an aspect of human interaction that I return to frequently, the bells that can't be unrung. The porousness of each of us, the way, at any given moment any other person we encounter, IRL or online, can change our lives through good intentions, ill intentions, or no intentions at all, in lasting and confusing ways. I think of a viral meme, a combination of tweets: the first one a group of frat-boy-coded young white men posing in the sun, the caption asking: "you see us all at the pool wyd" The response: "Killing myself in front of you to forever change your bond and the trajectory of your lives."[36]

We see car crashes halfway down the block, see smoking buildings on the television. People we've never met before put their hands on our bodies. Headlines on our feeds announce the news. Family members let slip unpleasant secrets. We are changed. *Built just like regular sentences, these sentences can in an instant forever change the life of their listeners.* There's no answer here. The unrhymed line a hanging emptiness.

Desire and the words we use to communicate it: *Will you marry me? I always thought that you and I had a little something between us. Are you doing anything later? I had a dream last night, and you were in it. Want to come in and have a drink? I'll show you mine if you show me yours.*

It, too, is a type of poem.

35 Chris Onstad, "May 22, 2007," Achewood, May 22, 2007, http://achewood.com/index.php?date=0522 2007.

36 "Killing Myself in Front of You to Forever Change Your Bond and the Trajectory of Your Lives," Know Your Meme, accessed April 8, 2025, https://knowyourmeme.com/memes/killing-myself-in-front-of-you-to-forever-change-your-bond-and-the-trajectory-of-your-lives.

Author's Note

Some passages in the book make use of a writing style that echoes the noticeably clipped narration of Gail Scott's *Furniture Music* (Wave Books, 2023). In *Post-Man,* these passages are intended to reflect the scattered, fast-paced thinking that sometimes accompanies ADHD.

Though this book comprises a number of essays written between 2014 and 2023, much of the writing and the bulk of its editing were done in 2024 and 2025, a period in which the use of large language models and generative AI was rampant. As someone politically, philosophically, spiritually, and emotionally opposed to AI, particularly in creative contexts, it was important to me not only not to use any AI in the writing of the book, but also to make the book a text that could not have been written by AI. Some of the project of this book was finding ways to create text that an AI would not.

Acknowledgments

Prior versions of these essays initially appeared in *Hazlitt, Maisonneuve, The Walrus, Catapult,* and *This Magazine*. Thank you to the editors at those publications.

Thank you to Brian and the whole team at Arsenal, for believing in this book and making the dream of it come true. To Catharine, for your sharpness and thoughtfulness and kindness with my work. To Jazmin, for going above and beyond to make the visual aspects of the book look as beautiful in real life as they did in my head.

To Carly, my agent, thank you for believing in this book and helping it find its home.

To Haley Cullingham and Tajja Isen, this book's two godmothers, thank you for accepting two pieces each, for two publications each, long before this book was an idea of mine, for the incredible boost those acceptances gave me in making me feel like a real writer.

Thank you to Tara-Michelle Ziniuk, for giving a piece about going bald outside the gender binary a home, and to andrea bennett and Erica Lenti, for very early editorial feedback on two of these essays.

Big thanks to Mom and Dad and Nat, for the love, the support, the kindness. For seeing and understanding me so well.

To Shuang and Jac and Olive and Raph and Laura and Mitch and Alyce and Dessa and Brian and Cat and Ali and EJ and all my wonderful friends, thank you for keeping me sane while I was writing this.

Thank you to everyone who's been a part of the stories that have made up my life so far, and thank you to you, for reading this.

Most of all, thank you to Blair, for editing, and for everything.

ALEX MANLEY is a non-binary writer, editor, and translator living and working in Montreal/Tiohtià:ke. They are the author of *The New Masculinity: A Roadmap for a 21st-Century Definition of Manhood* (ECW Press, 2023) and *We Are All Just Animals & Plants* (Metatron Press, 2016), a collection of poems. They are also the translator of *Made-Up: A True Story of Beauty Culture Under Late Capitalism* (Coach House Books, 2021), an English-language translation of Daphné B.'s *Maquillée*. Their work has appeared in publications like *Hazlitt*, *The Walrus*, *Maisonneuve*, *Catapult*, *This Magazine*, the *Literary Review of Canada*, *Electric Literature*, and Vulture, and they have been named a finalist for a National Magazine Award, a Digital Publishing Award, the Cole Foundation Prize for Translation, and the Mavis Gallant Prize for Non-Fiction. They are left-handed. ***alexmanley.com***